£ 2

CARDINAL
GORDON JOSEPH GRAY
A Biography

with best wishes,

Michael Turnbull

CARDINAL
GORDON JOSEPH GRAY
A Biography

Michael T R B Turnbull

SAINT ANDREW PRESS

EDINBURGH

First published in 1994 by
SAINT ANDREW PRESS
121 George Street, Edinburgh EH2 4YN.

Copyright © Michael T R B Turnbull 1994

ISBN 0 7152 0699 0

British Library Cataloguing in Publication Data
A catalogue record for this book
is available from the British Library.

ISBN 0 7152 0699 0

Cover design by Mark Blackadder.
Cover photograph and selected **photographs** in art section courtesy of Stewart Ferguson.

[Photograph sources in the art section have been acknowledged where known. If any source has been omitted, please inform the publisher for future acknowledgment.]

Printed and **bound** in Great Britain by Bell & Bain Ltd, Glasgow.

Contents

Foreword

IT is too soon to see the full significance of Archbishop Gordon Gray's elevation to the College of Cardinals, but a look at previous Cardinals connected with Scotland will perhaps put it into perspective.

Scottish Cardinals have always been rare birds. The first was Walter Wardlaw, Bishop of Glasgow (1367-87), who was a Cardinal for just three and a half years; and since the Avignon Pope who elevated him has been relegated by historians to the status of anti-pope, he does not count for the staunchly Roman Scottish Catholics of modern times.

Next came David Beaton, Archbishop of St Andrews (1539-46). A great statesman and patriot he may have been, but hardly a great example of priestly virtue.

Two later Cardinals bore Scottish names, though the career of each was in Italy, not Scotland. Henry Benedict (1725-1807), Duke of York and later, in Jacobite eyes, the rightful King Henry IX, was of the royal house of Stuart, but not since the birth of his great-grandfather Charles I at Dunfermline in 1600, had a royal Stuart of the direct line been born in Scotland.

Henry was born in Rome, as was Charles Erskine (1739-1811), son of a Scottish father and Italian mother. Formerly a student at the Scots College in Rome, Erskine visited Scotland as a Papal envoy in 1793 and was created a Cardinal in 1803.

Of the two Cardinals in this century, William Heard (1884-1973) was born in Edinburgh, where his father was headmaster of Fettes College. His career after leaving school was, however, entirely in England and Rome. He was, in fact, a priest of an English diocese.

The most recent Cardinal was, of course, Gordon Gray, Archbishop of St Andrews and Edinburgh (1951-85), who died only a few months ago.

Two near misses are recorded. George Conn (*c*. 1598-1640), born in Aberdeenshire, was Papal agent at the court of Charles I in London. The court's petition to have him created Cardinal was never granted.

The other, Peter Grant (1708-84), a Glenlivet man, was for forty-five years the agent of the Scottish clergy in Rome and a great favourite with English-speaking visitors. One Pope, it is said, intended to make him a Cardinal.

For completeness' sake, Cardinal George Innes can be added. Invented by apologists for the Trinitarian Order and Scottish Catholicism, he was said to be head of his order in fifteenth century Scotland. His portrait was painted—copies of it are to be found in Scotland—but he never actually walked on Planet Earth.

It is clear that, if Cardinals with Scottish connections are rare, Cardinals who lived their lives in Scotland are rarer still. Only two come into this category – David Beaton and Gordon Gray – and of Beaton it has to be said that not only were his education and political career to a great degree French, but he was also bishop of a French diocese.

Thus Gordon Gray emerges as the only Scottish Cardinal whose career was wholly Scottish and who can be classed as a pastoral-minded priest and bishop, rather than a diplomat or administrator. His entire life, apart from his seminary training in England, was spent in Scotland; he spoke no language other than English. This is possibly the most significant feature of his being a Cardinal.

Equally significant is something we do not yet know, for it is still in the future. Is Rome going to continue the pattern of creating Scottish Cardinals in an apparently haphazard fashion, or can we expect a Cardinal's hat to be given with some regularity to a Scottish diocesan bishop? Was Gordon Gray's elevation due solely to his personal qualities and his friendly relations with those in high places, or is he the first of a succession of Cardinals within the Scottish hierarchy?

Whatever the future holds, Gordon Joseph Gray was outstandingly successful as the first Cardinal resident in Scotland since the

Reformation, and Michael Turnbull's study lets us see why and how this was. The thirty-four years of his tenure of the diocese witnessed so many major challenges, making the Scottish Catholic Church in 1985 very different from what it had been in 1951, when he was appointed Archbishop.

Three developments can be singled out. The Roman Catholic Church in Scotland, which had been growing in almost every way for over a century, reached a peak in the 1960s and has since, as regards statistics, declined steeply. The Second Vatican Council in the 1960s inaugurated a new outlook and policy of dialogue between the Church and the world. Of course, any simplistic formula of cause and effect, whereby Vatican II is made responsible for the diminution of the Church, is clearly erroneous, for Scotland could not have remained exempt from the decline of Church allegiance throughout the western world, and Vatican II was an attempt to halt this decline.

The third development was the growth of Ecumenism. The voluntary isolation of Scottish Catholicism in the face of hostility gave way to increasing friendliness and co-operation with other Churches. Gordon Gray's position was very unlike that of his embattled predecessor in Edinburgh.

Michael Turnbull does not attempt to study these developments in depth, for they are too near to be seen in perspective. But to anyone wishing to follow the career of this great Church leader during the decades of radical challenge, I wholeheartedly recommend this book.

The Right Revd Mark Dilworth, OSB
~ Abbot of ST BENEDICT'S ABBEY, Fort Augustus ~

Introduction

INTENDED as a 'popular' life of Cardinal Gordon Joseph Gray, this biography is based primarily upon reminiscences which the Cardinal recorded within the last decade.

By their very nature, the memories he selects are fragmentary and may even appear idiosyncratic or banal, as he saw them fitfully through the veil of the intervening years. Those looking for a systematic or comprehensive account of the Second Vatican Council, for example, or of Cardinal Gray's work on the International Commission on English in the Liturgy, or a history of the Bauchi Mission, or a detailed analysis of archdiocesan administration, will be disappointed. Hopefully, more in-depth studies of the Cardinal's life and times will appear in the not-too distant future.

I first met Archbishop Gray – as he was then – in the mid-'50s, when I was still at school. The idea of writing his biography came to me in December 1992 and I went to see the Cardinal early in January 1993. Over the following months I wrote the first two chapters of the book and these were read, corrected and approved by him.

Cardinal Gray's personal records and the administrative records of his period in office as Archbishop of St Andrews and Edinburgh have recently been placed in the Scottish Catholic Archives in Edinburgh. According to standard archival practice, they remain closed to researchers for 30 or 100 years, depending on the sensitivity of the material. Nevertheless, these restrictions may in the future, at the discretion of the Church authorities, be lifted to allow advanced academic research to take place.

Consequently, a full and balanced assessment of the career of Cardinal Gray is not yet possible. Essentially, this biography is an attempt to capture the flavour of his life using such resources as were at my disposal.

Among the many who have helped me with advice and information are: Mr James P Armstrong; Father Bede Bailey; Monsignor John Barry; Monsignor James Brennan; Father Michael Burns; Mr Michael Burns of John S Burns & Sons; Father Tom Connelly; Bishop Mario Conti; Bishop Joseph Devine; Abbot Mark Dilworth; Father Thomas Engelen; Mr Tom Farmer; Father John Fitzsimmons; Monsignor Daniel Foley; Father Leo Glancy; Mr and Mrs George Gray and family; Sister Cyril Griffin; Father Reginald Hodgson; Father Ryszard Holuka; Father Michael Jackson; Dr Christine Johnson; Bishop Stephen McGill; Abbot Donald McGlynn; Father Andrew Monaghan; Archbishop Keith O'Brien; Canon James Rae; Mrs Agnes Wight; Archbishop Thomas Winning.

I am also most grateful to those who have contributed the appreciations which make up the appendix and to the Scottish Arts Council and the Winston Churchill Memorial Trust for refreshing my interest in biography.

Finally, I acknowledge gratefully the knowledge and experience acquired by my two years as East of Scotland correspondent for the *Scottish Catholic Observer*.

Michael T R B Turnbull

To my grandparents
~ Jessie and Bruce ~

CHAPTER 1

Beginnings

PASSING under the massive stone ropes knotted across the entrance to what was formerly Gillis College seminary in Edinburgh's leafy suburbs at Whitehouse Loan, the visitor would circle the northern end of the chapel and find himself in a hidden garden with lawns and gnarled fruit trees. Facing, was a small stone house, snugly furnished for retired Cardinal Gray.

Gordon Joseph, Cardinal Gray, first resident Scottish Cardinal since the Reformation, even in retirement, spoke a language that was plain, direct and unmistakably Scottish. The resonant bass rumbled like distant thunder, and with a power that once enabled him (in the days before churches were fitted with electric amplification) to be heard through the open door of St Mary's Cathedral as far as the foot of Leith Walk.

At the Hermitage, the visitors' book – crammed with the names of church leaders (such as the Dalai Lama) – was signed and then one was motioned close by the fire. In spite of suffering increasing infirmity – Bell's Palsy, then a severe heart-attack – the Cardinal was able to sit upright in his chair, his face craggy from a lifetime of action.

He would light up a cigarette with a single deceptive motion (even Princes of the Church are not above small failings) and slowly open up the pages of his life as if reading from a book.

Tradition asserts that his real family surname was 'Gordon'. But the Clan Gordon had been too involved in the Jacobite cause to be allowed to live in peace. After the '45 Rising, their name, like many others, was changed – to the less colourful 'Gray'. They were now the Grays of Marble Quarry, a landmark at Portsoy gouged from the rocky coast of the Moray Firth.

Sunday was the day of the week when the Gray family lifted their children into the pony trap and, the adults trudging beside them, rolled down the long road to Portsoy, and the little church of The Annunciation.

Like many a spunky Scots lad, his father set off down to Edinburgh in April 1887, looking to make his fortune. He was only 15, straight off his grandfather's farm at Cornhill in Banff, fresh off the land, still smelling of the family meal-mill, leaving behind him the warm faces of his brothers and sisters.

A man of few words, in time he was apprenticed as an engineer at Bertrams Ltd, the massive and gloomy works right beside the green open spaces of the Meadows. At their Sciennes Road premises, Bertrams produced heavy machinery for the paper-making industry and they exported all over the world.

In Edinburgh, Frank Gray found digs in Lothian Road. His first Sunday he crossed the Meadows to St Columba's, Upper Gray Street, not far from his work. Mass was a time to remember what he had left behind – family and farm, the windy coastline of Banff that seemed so much a part of his identity.

Emerging from Mass, Frank was met at the church door by Father Sandy Stuart, a native of Glenlivet, who still spoke with a peaty Highland accent. He took an almost fatherly interest in Frank and the two became life-long friends.

Frank worked out the long apprenticeship at Bertrams Ltd, with evening classes at the Heriot-Watt College, and then moved into design in the drawing-office before going to India in 1898 as chief engineer at a paper-mill near Calcutta.

Having contracted malaria, he returned to Scotland in 1902 and rejoined the design staff in Bertrams Works at Sciennes.

Not long after, he met Angela Jane Oddy, a young schoolteacher at the Catholic school in Glen Street. She had been given a sound start in life at the Convent of Notre Dame, and by the Ursuline nuns at St Margaret's Seminary in Marchmont. Angela Oddy had dark hair and a quiet but luminous personality. They decided to get married and found a house in Bellevue on the north-east of the city, not far from St Mary's Cathedral. Shortly after their marriage in 1904, Father Stuart was appointed administrator at the Cathedral, in due course being made a Canon.

The first two children were born at Bellevue – Josephine and George. There was further celebration in the Gray household when, in 1909, Frank Gray earned promotion to the post of works manager at James Bertram & Son, Leith Walk – a firm engaged in designing paper-mills, many for Sweden and India. The Gray family took up residence at the works manager's house next to the site.

Frank Gray was an outstanding engineer and designer in his own specialised field. Not long afterwards he was made managing director. In the early 1930s, both firms came to a joint working arrangement and Frank Gray became a director of both firms.

Gordon Gray was born on 10th August 1910. When he was about three years old, the family moved to Dudley Terrace, not far from the historic fishing and ship-building village of Newhaven and the Port of Leith. They were now parishioners of Our Lady, Star of the Sea.

About 1917 the Grays moved again, this time to Newhaven Road, to a roomy, four-floored terraced house which they bought from the owner of a trawler fleet, Tom Devlin.

For Mrs Gray the house was something of a nightmare to run – even with the help of a maid and an occasional 'daily'. Fortunately the house had been modernised, including the large basement with wash-house and coal cellar. The kitchen was converted into a well-fitted workshop, which included a six-foot lathe.

There young Gordon Gray spent many happy hours developing a life-long passion for working with metal and wood. In the front and back gardens, he also nurtured a love for gardening.

His father was often abroad supervising the construction of paper-mills, especially in India where he pioneered the use of quick-growing bamboo to be turned into pulp for the manufacture of paper.

When he was away on business, the whole Gray family prayed for his safety by reciting the Rosary. Mrs Gray and her children often went to the Convent of Marie Reparatrice nearby, to hear daily Mass and attend the service of Benediction, with its litanies, hymns and incense.

Gordon Gray became an altar server at the age of about six, trained by the nuns to know the Latin responses by heart and carry the heavy Roman missal (with its thick black text and blood-red *rubrics* or directions) from one side of the altar to the other without tripping!

Around 1915, like the other Gray children, he started at Holy Cross Primary School, close to home and just across the road from the Convent of Marie Reparatrice.

Along with Holy Cross Secondary School, which stood on the same site, the Primary was the result of the efforts of Archbishop James Smith, whose begging and borrowing campaign had brought in the funds needed to buy the site of an old mansion house.

The Archbishop's aim had been to open a school which would prepare young Catholics to enter the professions – teaching in particular.

The first Rector of Holy Cross Secondary was Dr Alexander Cran. He was not a Catholic himself, but a man dedicated to the service of education. He respected Archbishop Smith's hopes for the future of the school and never forgot his vision of a *katholikos* (holistic) community.

At Holy Cross all the classrooms were small and cold. The art room was housed in an old Victorian glass conservatory. The science room was set up in the stables and the technical classroom in the gardener's shed. In the basement kitchen was the dining hall. There the main course was a penny plate of lentil soup.

Before and after school, and in the middle break, there was one escape from this ravaged landscape – the convent across the road, where, for a few minutes, pupils and staff could pray before the Blessed Sacrament, the body of Christ exposed among flickering candles and fragrant flowers in a sunburst of gold.

Educational methods then were old-fashioned by today's standards.

'We learned the three Rs by rote,' remembered Cardinal Gray. 'We memorised each answer in the Penny Catechism as well as all our basic prayers.'

The children learned at an age when memory was highly retentive. If Gordon Gray and his fellow scholars did not always know the meaning of some of the Catechism answers, they at least knew the definitions off by heart and would come to understand them in later years.

As the Gray children grew up into secondary pupils, religious instruction in church on Sunday was replaced by the often tedious Sunday sermon which paraphrased the words of the Gospel, in many cases, thought Gordon, vastly weakening the message of Christ.

'I am still convinced,' adds Cardinal Gray, 'that the old methods were the best. Modern techniques of teaching religion too often produce a woolly and inaccurate understanding of the fundamentals.'

Newhaven Road was in a prosperous residential area from which the neighbouring children went mostly to the Merchant Company schools.

'Like our Catholic contemporaries,' recalls Cardinal Gray, 'we were shunned as a foreign and alien religious group. We were God's peculiar people. No open hostility. We were not worth bothering about. For Catholics such as ourselves, life was simple but comfortable. It was only when one of our number attempted to become socially acceptable in the better circles of Edinburgh society that any real hostility would be felt. We existed happily, untroubled, content – a community centred around our nearest parish.'

At Holy Cross Secondary a new Rector succeeded Dr Cran. Sandy Paterson, from Enzie in Morayshire, presided over still primitive accommodation.

Holy Cross Academy expanded and developed. Through the efforts of John Gordon and Louis Byrne, a rugby team was born and fixtures found.

'We played our next-door neighbours Trinity Academy, and then the Royal High School, Heriot's, and the rest,' the Cardinal recollects. 'We had stepped out of the catacombs – a very gentle ecumenical step, now unrecognised and forgotten – yet, looking back over the years, significant I believe. It was no longer Hibs and Hearts, Celtic and Rangers. We were Holy Cross Rugby Team, ready for any challenge in our grade. There never was any sectarianism in rugby – unlike soccer.'

Along with home and school, the institution of the Church

played an important part in helping young people like Gordon Gray to grow into mature Christians.

On Sundays there was early Mass in the convent; then up to the parish church – St Mary's Cathedral – for Solemn High Mass in which the haunting tones of plainchant and the interwoven textures of polyphony combined with heady incense to waft the believer almost to paradise.

There was a bewildering variety of liturgies – Benediction, with the priest swathed in a cope of gold; the painful pilgrimage through the Stations of the Cross; the Rosary, with its hypnotic prayer and comforting massage of beads.

In 1922, Father Cuthbert Chase was appointed the first pastor of the newly-formed parish of Holy Cross. He took over the convent chapel as his church until a new building could be put up three years later.

Father Chase became diocesan inspector of schools and also diocesan master of ceremonies. He was very popular with his altar boys, but he was a hard man.

He had a passion for ceremonial and drilled the altar boys for their parts in the liturgy as if they were in the Guards. But he was a real friend to Gordon Gray and the other altar boys, with his boyish enthusiasm, his never-empty bag of sweets and the chance of a spin on his three-speed bicycle.

A second sister, Peggy, had been born. In 1925, when she was six, she contracted scarlet fever. Gordon was the only one in the Gray family who had not been attacked by what was then a life-threatening illness.

If Gordon was to stay in the house with his parents, said the family doctor, then Peggy would have to go to an isolation hospital. Father Chase resolved the problem by arranging for her brother to stay with him in the Holy Cross presbytery at Denham Green Place.

Gordon stayed there for a memorable six weeks. Father Chase was more than kind to him, as was his housekeeper, Barbara Carter. He took Gordon everywhere – on calls to the sick for comfort and consolation in their illness; to the cinema with its dark mystery; even on his first trip to the merchant city of Glasgow, the 'dear green place'.

Father Chase kept the lad busy – leading the prayers each morning during the month of October (devoted to the Virgin Mary); constructing a charging-board for the Canon's radio accumulator or designing a new easy-assembly Christmas crib; even (after laborious measurement) a catafalque for All Souls' Day (2nd November).

In the years that followed there were happy days almost without exception, without compulsion, where the boy learned by Father Chase's example what a priest's life is and the satisfaction that priesthood can bring.

It was his uncle, Canon John Alan Gray, who first directly approached his nephew about the priesthood. He was parish priest in Dunfermline, Fife when, early one summer, he invited Gordon over the Forth for a few days, in order to help him clear a mountain of cinders and ashes from the boilerhouse under the church.

Out of the blue the Canon announced that in the evening he and Gordon would go down to a little loch not too far outside the town on which he had fishing rights. The loch was plagued with pike that spoiled the trout fishing.

'We made wooden floats – otters – to which lines and hooks baited with herring were fastened,' Cardinal Gray remembered. 'These were to be left overnight to catch the pike and we would return in the morning. We set out by car from Dunfermline, loaded up with a new outboard motor (which my uncle had just bought for the ten-foot dinghy), the floats and a two-gallon can of petrol. The car was left at the farm and, weighted down, we made our way to the boat. There was a gentle breeze, so he told me we could safely drift out.

'One by one, we unravelled the lines, put the otters into the water and then prepared to row ashore. But – he had forgotten the oars, they were in the farm steading.

'It didn't matter. We had the outboard motor. We fixed it to the boat, filled the tank, primed the carburettor and pulled the starter rope. Silence. It wouldn't start .... The slight breeze had died down,' continues the Cardinal. 'Darkness had fallen – a wonderful setting for quiet, serious thought. We took it.

'What was I going to do when I left school? I was then well

past 16 with only the rest of the summer term to go. Eventually he broached the subject of the priesthood.

'I told him that it was, I thought, what I wanted. He tried to steer me in the direction of a religious Order (the Jesuits in particular) saying that the Orders (with their communities and companionship to support the individual) enjoyed advantages over the secular priest who had to contend with loneliness, isolation and one-man responsibility.

'But I made it clear,' concluded the Cardinal with a wry smile, 'that if I had a vocation, I felt it was to the diocesan clergy and to the archdiocese of St Andrews and Edinburgh. We left it at that. And I think he was pleased.'

CHAPTER 2

Seminary Days

GORDON Gray took the decision to study for the priesthood, but he was in a bit of a quandary. James Smith, the Archbishop of St Andrews and Edinburgh at the time, was blind and housebound. In effective charge of the archdiocese was the Presbyterian convert, auxiliary Bishop Grey Graham (1874-1959) who had an inflexible rule that any student with a relative already a priest in the diocese, was not to be accepted as a student for the archdiocese at Blairs College, near Aberdeen. The Bishop had a scrupulous fear of nepotism.

Fortunately the Grays' parish priest, Father Chase, offered a possible solution. He was English, born in Chelsea, and at the age of eleven had become a Catholic. He decided to be a priest and went to St John's Seminary in Wonersh, Surrey, which catered for both junior and senior boys.

'For some reason which I never discovered,' adds Cardinal Gray, 'Father Chase had applied to be accepted by the archdiocese of St Andrews and Edinburgh. In due course he was sent to complete his studies at the Scots College in Rome. But his health broke down. He returned to Wonersh to finish his Theology course and was ordained in 1905 at Southwark Cathedral.'

Father Chase had loved Wonersh College and its regime. He knew Gordon Gray probably would be rejected by Bishop Graham because his uncle was a priest in the diocese. Instead he strongly advised Mr and Mrs Gray to send their son to Wonersh. They were delighted.

So, on their son's behalf, Father Chase wrote off and discovered that the junior section of the College had since moved to new premises at Mark Cross in East Sussex, five miles south of

Tunbridge Wells, which by then housed some 70 boys aged between 12 and 19.

'Archbishop Peter Amigo,' recalled the Cardinal, 'had ruled that students straight from school should pass at least one year in the Junior College. I landed up at St Joseph's, Mark Cross in September 1927 and, owing to the examination system (which led to a London University degree) spent two years there.'

He was taken down to England on the night train by Father Chase. This left time to see London in a day – from Westminster Cathedral to the Tower of London. In the late afternoon they took the train from Victoria, got off at the nearest station and went on to the College by road.

'We were welcomed by Monsignor Ernest Corbishley, a kindly man, who enjoyed indifferent health. But he was tough and ruled with a rod of iron. I soon discovered that the regime was equally tough – much tougher even, I imagine, than the noviciate of any religious Order.

'I was privileged, I learned, to be brought in with Father Chase for a cup of tea with the staff. Then I was shown my cubicle, handed my College prayer book and left to fend for myself.

'The only other Scot, a student from Clydebank called Tom McKenna, took pity on me, showed me the geography of the house and gave me an idea of the daily timetable. I was a stranger in a strange land.'

The daily routine was not easy. Every morning at five to six the rising bell sounded and the boys were expected to be in chapel twenty minutes later for morning prayers. Private meditation followed, broken only by the intoning of three short scriptural quotations, designed to focus the boys' sleepy thoughts. At seven sharp came Mass, which filled the hungry imagination with images of sin and salvation.

After Mass, private thanksgiving followed which, as Cardinal Gray remembered long after, 'on an empty stomach seemed an eternity!'

Then the boys marched in single file to the refectory for a breakfast of tea, bread and margarine. Mealtime was one of the few opportunities when silence could be broken and the most was made of the opportunity, the hall echoing with animated chatter.

Breakfast over, it was time to make beds and visit the toilet before assembling in the study-hall, each boy at his desk, to hear notices before class.

Classes, interrupted only by a ten minute break, went on until quarter to one, when the boys again filed into the chapel for particular examen (a time to assess, each in his heart, the state of his conscience, his relationship with God and with others). Lunch was the high point of the day – a solid three-course meal consisting usually of a very thin soup, good meat with plenty of potatoes and vegetables. The sweets ranged from rice or tapioca to satisfying steam-puddings and wonderful apple dumplings.

Next came another visit to the chapel, to the Blessed Sacrament, the Body of Christ proclaimed by a candle burning in a red glass lamp. The host was reverently enclosed in a container of gold sheltered on the altar in a small tabernacle – a miniature tent.

High spirits filled the recreation time until two o'clock when, except on Sundays and two free afternoons each week, classes resumed until four. Free afternoons were for football, hockey or cricket (depending on the time of year) or an organised 'crocodile' walk.

What pocket money the boys had was given up at the beginning of term. Soap, stamps, envelopes and other items had to be bought 'on tick' at the College shop. Gordon Gray was rather fortunate. Perhaps at the suggestion of Father Chase, he was appointed as College carpenter with an outhouse workshop to himself. Except for Sundays, when he was forced to play organised games (much to the disapproval of his Scottish sabbatarian turn of mind!) he could legitimately dodge games and devote his time to replacing football studs or flattening out protruding nails in walking-shoes.

Later still – when it was realised that he could tackle other more complicated jobs, mending desks or making seating from old gymnasium wall-bars to put around the cricket field – he acquired a privileged position, free to avoid games at will.

Tea-time was the next landmark in the College day. Its menu was similar to breakfast. It preceded 'prep', a time for homework and revision, ended at seven o'clock.

This was the time to assemble in the Oratory for a talk on matters spiritual, perhaps a commentary on the College Rule or on a book, and then the Rosary – Hail Marys recited in cycles of meditation. Sometimes it was Benediction, when hymns were sung before the Blessed Sacrament, and burning incense was offered by a priest robed in a glittering vestment, with embroidered letters and images in rich colour.

As the day drew to a close, the boys were allowed another half hour of recreation, then free study, more prep, letter-writing or reading in the study-hall. Nine o'clock prayers was the final duty before bed.

Since Gordon knew no Greek, he was directed to study History for the London Matriculation exam. This he did on his own, unsupervised. It proved to be a fruitful exercise as he had to work out his own course and timetable from old Matriculation papers.

The first holiday for the boys came on St John's Day, 27th December, after a real English Christmas. Gordon had ten days to spend at home. His parents had by this time moved from Leith to a splendid house with a large garden at Eskbank, Dalkeith, just south of Edinburgh. Next door was St David's Church.

It was a longed-for return home after the traumatic experience of being away for four months – especially as the long unbroken session loomed ahead, stretching right through to July.

But because of the strict regime, he had little time to weary. He enjoyed it, taking each day as it came. Liturgical feasts free of classes made the long weeks more bearable. Every boy counted the days till the long summer break.

In the second year Gordon was given a black cassock which buttoned right up the front, and a biretta which he wore somewhat self-consciously on his head. They were presented to him at a service in church and thereafter he wore them, as the custom was, all day, except when going for walks or on the odd occasions when he had to play games.

Other privileges given to the more senior boys included that of being a server at table. This meant that, after the meal, they could enjoy in peace what food remained after the other boys had left. It also included all the left-overs from the Rector's table, which the nuns who ran the kitchen sometimes kindly augmented.

Looking back from the vantage-point of later years, Cardinal Gray judged the system to be an excellent trial for a vocation, although very hard for the young boys.

'Spiritually, I can now see some gaps. We had no spiritual director, only a choice of the priests on the staff as confessors. There was no real instruction on mental prayer, nor a better appreciation of the Sacrament of Penance. There were no classes in religious education. But, with the Priesthood as the great objective, one was ready to accept whatever the years of preparation might demand.'

In July 1929 Gordon Gray finished at Mark Cross. The following September he began his course of studies at St John's Seminary, Wonersh, three miles south-east of Guildford. Its regime was the traditional senior seminary one, an easier and more flexible life than that at Mark Cross, and appropriately modified for a more mature level of student.

There was a strange mixture of men in Gordon Gray's first year class – among others, a former Thames bargee (who, being completely bald, faced Archbishop Amigo with a problem when he was presented to have his hair shaved for the tonsure), and an ex-soldier who had lost his leg in the First World War.

During their first year, students were housed in the cubicles off the old junior college, with one concession to the times – where a curtain had once been, there was now a door. Fish-tailed gas burners in the corridor provided the only artificial light. If students wanted to study in their cubicles, they had to provide their own lighting. Gordon Gray brought a good incandescent paraffin lamp from home and so was able to live and study in reasonable comfort. There was the same rising bell as at Mark Cross, but it rang half an hour later. The study programme was similar to that of a university – three lectures a day, each lasting one hour and periods of private study. Afternoons were free until four o'clock.

Pipe-smoking was allowed during recreation – but not cigarettes. The food was of the same uneven quality as that at Mark Cross, with one difference – jam or marmalade could be eaten, as long as students provided it at their own expense.

The toilet accommodation, on the ground floor, was pre-

Victorian! No water cisterns, only earth boxes which a farm-hand refilled every day. The students washed in cold water, having the luxury of a bath of tepid water only once a week in rotation.

After lunch the afternoons at Wonersh were free for games or work until four o'clock. This arrangement suited Gordon admirably. In the winter there were roses to prune, the workshop for odd jobs and (a new hobby) book-binding.

In the summer he had hives of bees to manage, rustic fencing to repair and the cemetery to look after. Then there was swimming in the College's own little pool, or rowing on the canal, or walks on the Sussex Downs.

There was no training in pastoral theology, except for a meticulous attention to liturgical worship which included voice production and preaching – the latter to fellow-students, the most daunting of audiences.

As at Mark Cross, there was no specialised spiritual director, but most evenings there was a *lecture spirituel* led by the Rector, Monsignor Mallett. There were two years of two lectures a day in Thomistic Philosophy.

'It seemed more or less unintelligible,' recalled Cardinal Gray later, 'a waste of time then – but we were to realise its value when we began our studies in Theology.'

The years passed quickly. By the end of his second year Gordon had not been *incardinated* (that is, formally accepted as a student for the priesthood of a particular diocese). Archbishop Amigo, eager as every archbishop is for new recruits, sent for him and told him he would accept him for Southwark and give him a bursary to the English College in Rome.

'I think there was a twinkle in his eye,' Cardinal Gray observed in hindsight. 'I think he liked me, since he always addressed me as "You old Scotchman!" which I rather resented because of the "ch".'

In the event, Gordon informed Archbishop Amigo that he wanted to work in Scotland and the Archbishop gave him his blessing. Gordon then wrote to Archbishop McDonald in Edinburgh who officially recognised his canonical position.

He received all his Orders (porter, lector, exorcist and acolyte) along with the sub-diaconate and the diaconate from the hands of

Archbishop Amigo, but after the pre-ordination retreat he returned to Edinburgh, stayed the night there at Cathedral House and was ordained next day, 15th June 1935, by one of the greatest Scottish Bishops, Archbishop Andrew Joseph McDonald (1871-1950) a Benedictine monk, formerly Abbot of Fort Augustus in Inverness-shire.

St Mary's Cathedral, standing at the windy top of Edinburgh's Leith Walk, was crowded for the Mass, with many friends from Dalkeith. Afterwards Gordon and his family went for a private meal in the nearby George Hotel. As guests of the family came Archbishop McDonald, Father Chase and his housekeeper who had looked after him as a guest in Holy Cross presbytery.

In those days the custom was that the newly-ordained priest stayed 'in retreat' until after his first Mass. Gordon's family respected this tradition and he retired to his room at the Knoll, Eskbank, until Sunday 16th June when he celebrated his first Mass – which of course was really his second!

In those days there were no parochial parties or presentations. He offered Mass at Holy Cross where he preached his first sermon. Another Mass was in the local Convent of the Sisters of Mercy in Eskbank, and a third in the medieval kitchen of Newbattle Abbey which had been converted by the Lothian family into a small chapel.

'I can recall little else,' Cardinal Gray said, 'except a brief word from the Archbishop that I was appointed to St Andrews University in Fife to study for a degree and serve as a curate – at that time the Archbishop held university degrees for priests to be essential, so that they might have academic parity with school-teachers. I do not agree with his theory in this matter. A well-ordered and well-followed seminary course is far more demanding intellectually than an Ordinary or even an Honours degree.'

CHAPTER 3

The Curate

GORDON Gray acted as a supply priest for three weeks at Holy Cross in Edinburgh to allow Father Chase to return to Wonersh for his annual retreat, and – contrary to his normal practice – take a few days' holiday.

In Scotland, meanwhile, sectarianism of a violent nature had raised its head: in the West through Alexander Ratcliff, founder of the Scottish Protestant League and a Dennistoun town councillor; in the East through John Cormack, leader of the Protestant Action Society, who soon won for himself and his followers six or seven seats on Edinburgh Town Council.

It came to a head in June 1935 when Archbishop McDonald organised a diocesan Eucharistic Congress in Edinburgh. There were months preceding the event during which church windows were stoned and broken, ugly graffiti was daubed on buildings and pavements, and priests, religious and lay Catholics were molested and attacked.

Councillor Cormack presided over a large gathering of several thousand people on Calton Hill under the auspices of Protestant Action. The Councillor produced a large knife which he drew from its sheath, saying that he had seen it in the hands of a Roman Catholic woman who claimed she was going to use it to prevent him from speaking at the Usher Hall that night.

Alexander Cameron of the Scottish Reformation Society preached from the pulpit of the Guthrie Memorial Church, saying that the Eucharistic Congress was the first ever held in Scotland. It was the most conspicuous affront, he claimed, that could be offered to the Protestant citizens of Edinburgh, the leading Protestant city in the world.

When the Congress was in its second day, a mass rally of women was held in Waverley Market. Thousands of Cormack's followers, with adherents from the West and Northern Ireland, closed in on the Market.

Police were out in force, including all the mounted police that could be mustered.

Gordon and his brother George, who had taken the car to pick up their mother and sister, Josephine, could get no nearer than George Street. Thousands of screaming, fanatical Cormack followers surged forward in waves, only to roll back again as the mounted police drove down upon them.

George Gray recalled the incident clearly:

'I drove my mother up there. My father and Gordon came with me. We let my mother off to go into the Waverley Market and we stood on the other side of the road.

'When the meeting was finished and the women came out to get into buses and coaches, a terrible noise started, abuse was being thrown at them; there was hammering on windows, the sound of breaking glass, and my father, who was standing between Gordon and myself, on the other side of the road, said in his quiet way – "I've travelled all over the world. I've lived among natives and savages but I've never seen people behave like *this!*" As he said that, the crowd turned on him. Gordon got him round one side, I got the other, and managed to get him down a side street with the help of the police.'

Eventually, the women came out from their gathering and for their return home were shepherded into buses with shattered windows, dented with stones.

The same scenes were enacted next evening around the grounds of the Benedictine Priory School at Canaan Lane, Morningside, where a procession of the Blessed Sacrament made up of some 1,200 persons took place before 10,000 worshippers. In the centre of the grass was the high altar, with four tall pillars in red, black and gold, standing on a gold base resting on a white platform.

The Priory, however, was in a virtual state of siege by the police. Members of the Protestant Action Society walked up and down with placards and shouts of 'No Popery!' resounded. There were clashes between the demonstrators and the police for over a mile down Morningside Road, with Councillor Cormack apparently urging people to preserve order and to disperse quietly.

After the service was over, buses passing Holy Corner were hit by missiles and the police had to make a baton-charge. Buses were not only stoned, but overturned, and a great deal of fighting ensued, especially on Bruntsfield Links as the demonstrators headed back to the City centre.

Gordon Gray recalled the event clearly – he was leading the procession and carrying the processional cross. The Priory School was only four or five hundred yards from Archbishop's House. The event brought back memories of Bishop George Hay who had looked down on a dark February night in 1779 to his little church in Chalmer's Close, Edinburgh, set ablaze by a riotous mob screaming, 'we are burning down the Papist church and looking for the Papist Bishop to put on top of the blaze!'

A letter in *The Scotsman* (22nd June 1935) caught the general revulsion of members of the Church of Scotland at Councillor Cormack's activities, and the writer urged ministers to condemn the violence openly from their pulpits: 'Few Presbyterians in Edinburgh approve of the recent conduct of certain active Protestants in showing their dislike of functions in which Roman Catholics took part. Doubtless some of the noisy zealots are not connected with any organised Church, but the disgrace of their actions falls on the whole body of Presbyterians.'

However, in spite of the gradual lessening of violent sectarian opposition, there still remained, at that time and for some years to come, institutionalised opposition in Scotland which prevented Catholics rising to the higher ranks of commerce or the professions.

Towards the middle of June 1935, Father Gray (as he had become) took the train across the Forth Bridge to St Andrews. From the station he was conveyed by horse-drawn cab to the presbytery at the Scores, right beside the golf links and the white sands which stretched as far as the eye could see.

'My uncle was at home, when I arrived,' Cardinal Gray remembered, 'and welcomed me in his own warm and casual way. We were old friends. I was a youngster when he came home on leave as an Army chaplain during the First World War. I had knelt at his feet to unlace his leggings.'

Canon John Gray was from Portsoy in Banffshire. He started life as a grain-miller, then decided to become a priest and trained at the Scots College in Rome. But he had an extraordinary technical bent – not only had he won the Military Cross at the Western Front during the First World War, but he had also designed (and used in field operations) a machine for administering nitrous oxide gas and oxygen to patients on the operating table. In his presbytery he had installed a burglar detector, while among his spare-time passions was clock-repairing.

Both men had much in common – woodwork, metalwork, gardening, bee-keeping and much more. To all who visited him, the Canon gave a warm, friendly welcome – holiday-makers, priests, university intellectuals, farm-workers. He was able to talk to all of them on their own wave-length. Above all, he could communicate with children. They loved him with simple affection and trust.

His uncle showed Gordon how to teach children religion in their own homes – usually farm-workers' cottages. Canon Gray always carried a bag filled with bars of chocolate for the children who knew their Catechism answers. Needless to say, they all did.

And there were other lessons too – he met an old cabinet-maker, a man who really loved his craft:

'I wanted to make a bookcase,' remembered the Cardinal, 'and my idea was to nail planks of wood together. Under his guidance, however, it eventually took me four months to put together. Shoddy work was not for him. He taught me some of his skills and it was a joy to learn. There were no nails or screws – only good dovetail joints.'

Some time before Gordon arrived in St Andrews, his uncle had begun to celebrate Mass in an Italian ice-cream shop in a picturesque fishing village ten miles south of St Andrews – Pittenweem.

This had been started through the assistance of an American priest who had been taking a short course at St Andrews University and who helped Canon Gray on Sundays. With the arrival of Gordon Gray, a regular Mass at Pittenweem became possible.

Then Milton House at Pittenweem came on the market. An anonymous benefactor and Gordon Gray's father bought it for the archdiocese in August 1935 – in spite of a little local opposition, which included a few broken windows.

With his uncle, Gordon set to work. They planned to make two of the downstairs rooms into a chapel. With the help of a number of local men, the two priests took away the dividing walls. Gordon was holding one of the beams up on his shoulders, when the unthinkable happened – he was seen slowly sinking under the weight of the beam and was only rescued in the nick of time! Fortunately, after this initial crisis, all went well, and late in September Canon Gray began a regular Sunday Mass in Pittenweem.

At first it was a congregation of between 20 and 30 who came from Colinsburgh, St Monance, Elie, Kilconquar and Anstruther, as well as the Durkins – a wonderful family from Pittenweem.

Gordon Gray was given special responsibility for Pittenweem with its scattered congregation – an apostolate he was much more inclined to than studying for his university degree!

For his Archbishop, the degree course was the greater priority. Father Gordon matriculated, bought his undergraduate gown and, not a little embarrassed by the flamboyant red garment, went to see his director of studies to arrange his course of lectures.

'Feeling very self-conscious in the scarlet gown and Roman collar,' he recalled years later to a group of undergraduates at St Andrews, 'I walked along in the shadow of the wall of St Leonard's to my first lecture.'

Father Gordon had decided to go for Honours and arrived for his first lecture, by Professor Blyth Webster on English Literature. Professor Webster knew his material, spoke without hesitation and with the most exquisite diction. He gripped the attention of even the most unreceptive student. During his third lecture he suddenly addressed Gordon as 'Father Gray'. Thereafter the ice was broken and his fellow-students accepted the young priest and knew what to call him courteously.

Father Gray was to meet one of those students many years later, when he was living in retirement. Bob Craig – today Professor Robert Craig – former Moderator of the General Assembly of the Church of Scotland, paid a courtesy call on the Cardinal in August 1986 when he was living in retirement at the Hermitage.

In the first two years, Gordon studied English, Latin, General Science, History, Logic and Metaphysics. In his final (Honours) year the subject was English Language and Literature, and the class numbered only three.

In any event, it was the parish which was Gordon's joy, young and zealous as he was. It was his first love. As his lectures normally took place between nine and eleven in the morning and five in the afternoon, he could be picked up by his uncle at eleven and was dropped off either at the church in Pittenweem or for Catechism visits elsewhere.

A good friend of his, Dr Jonathan Tate, a lecturer in Greek, advised him to organise his private study with a minimum of three real hours of study a day. Gordon took his advice and usually kept ten o' clock to one in the morning for peace and study. This sufficed, although sometimes it was a struggle and parish work had to take priority.

The years passed happily, though sometimes anxiously when exams loomed ahead. There were few Catholic students at St Andrews. Including those who travelled from Dundee, there were only seven.

As the final examinations approached in 1939, Professor Webster wrote to Archbishop McDonald asking him to free Gordon from parish duties to allow him to concentrate on his revision. The Archbishop did not reply.

Canon Gray was ill at the time and had gone to Rome to recuperate. Gordon faced eleven three-hour papers – six hours a day. He asked if the Archbishop would dispense him from the daily recitation of the Divine Office (matins, lauds, prime, terce, sext, none, vespers and compline, which would take around one and a quarter hours to work through) and commute it to other oral prayers, but the Archbishop replied that he did not have the authority to do so.

During the period of his finals Gordon was alone for a month, carrying out pastoral work at St Andrews and Pittenweem. The outcome was that he passed with a good Second Class Honours degree, but not with the First of which Professor Webster had thought him capable. He was the first Catholic priest to have graduated from St Andrews since the Reformation.

Shortly afterwards Gordon received word to proceed to Strawberry Hill College of Education in London to study Catechetics and also to work with Frank Sheed lecturing in Hyde Park for the Catholic Evidence Guild.

However, the War broke out in September 1939. Strawberry Hill was evacuated out of London and Gordon was a free man.

Then Archbishop McDonald proposed that he should take a Diploma in Education at Dundee. Gordon went to see the Principal there, Professor McLelland, not a Catholic but a wise adviser to the Church. He counselled against such a project unless Gordon could be freed from all parish work.

That was impossible, since, with the outbreak of hostilities, St Andrews (a large parish territorially) was flooded with children who had been evacuated from the populated areas of the Lothians. There were over a thousand children from Edinburgh and Lothian Catholic schools. Finally, the Archbishop capitulated and dropped the idea of still more academic qualifications.

Gordon was delighted. But, all his male student contemporaries had been called up for military service and he wanted to follow them.

He asked to be allowed to offer himself as a chaplain to the Forces. The Archbishop refused, saying that he had more than enough to do with the evacuees. Four times in all Gordon tried. Then the senior RAF chaplain, Monsignor Beauchamp, visited St Andrews and told him he was short of chaplains. 'What about it?' he asked.

Gordon told him to write to the Archbishop. He did, and received a terse postcard telling him to do his own job and leave Father Gray alone. That was his final refusal. So Father Gray settled down and accepted the decision ....

All the country districts became his special responsibility – from Elie to St Andrews and a few farms in the Cupar and Guardbridge areas. He changed his push-bike for an Excelsior Autocycle, bought oilskins and rubber leggings to cover the scattered district in fair weather and foul. Gordon's exploits on his autocycle were legendary – like the occasion when he appeared over the hill from St Andrews on his way to Mass at Pittenweem. He was late and it was snowing heavily. In his hurry to reach the church he was unable to use his brakes and was obliged to stop by falling off his vehicle into a ditch.

Pittenweem was the centre around which most of the evacuees and teachers were lodged. There were regular week-day Masses, Benediction and two Sunday Masses in the little church – and Rosary every afternoon.

Canon Lawrence Glancey, at that time a student for the priesthood in his final year, recalls 'my mother protested at people who expected their priest to face the rigorous conditions of blinding rain and snow-bound roads in order to say a week-day Mass. Father Gray never complained, as he unpeeled two or three coats, as many gloves and helmets and dried himself out before Mass.

'He had,' continues Canon Glancey, 'a great devotion to St Thérèse of Lisieux. He actually made the little shrine in Pittenweem, complete with an iron bracket with tiny holders for flowers all around. He and his uncle were very keen on flowers for the altar, and they grew most of them themselves.'

The small East Neuk seaside village had become popular as a family holiday resort. Many Catholics came from the West of Scotland, bringing a much needed injection of fervour to the little local flock who, for so long, had been starved of Catholic schooling and worship.

The two priests came to expect a full church for every week-day Mass in the summer and they were never disappointed. Gordon's parents loved Pittenweem and the surrounding area, so each year his mother and father rented a house in the village and he enjoyed glorious working holidays staying with them.

In the winter the work was heavy – with wartime lighting restrictions and blackouts. Riding an autocycle on wintry roads, with the tiny permitted glimmer of light, was a strain. But, catechising in farm cottages and a crowded chapel for every service at Pittenweem (even with the shaded light of a couple of candles) was an uplifting experience.

Gradually the children returned home, but some remained with one teacher to care for them – Mary Curran. With the Durkins, she was a co-founder of the parish.

A year after the War had started, a Fleet Air Arm unit was stationed at Crail. Since an air landing strip had to be built, there was an sudden influx of labourers, who were mainly Irish.

Gordon started a Mass in Aird's Hall, on week days a licensed dance hall. On Sundays it exuded an odour, not of sanctity, but of tobacco smoke and stale beer. However, the men turned up to church in force.

Some months later came the first air raid. One bomb fell on waste land, a second in a field behind a fine redstone Protestant church which was used for storing that valuable wartime commodity — wastepaper. Stones and even boulders were hurled up into the air, and some fell through the roof of the old church.

Canon Gray was quick off the mark. The building was no longer required, so he offered around £200 for it and his offer was accepted. The roof was patched up, Gordon and his uncle spent some of their own time tidying up and repairing the interior, and soon after it came into use as a second chapel of ease.

In mid-July 1941 Archbishop McDonald called at St Andrews. As Gordon was out of town at the time, he left a message with the Canon.

Gordon returned to be met by his uncle who sat him down, poured out an unaccustomed gin and martini and delivered the message. Gordon had been appointed parish priest at Hawick in the Borders.

'I think he was sad,' Cardinal Gray recalled many years later, 'so in a way was I. But, after all — what young priest is not thrilled at the thought of taking charge of his own parish.'

Father Gray left St Andrews on the morning of 15th August 1941 driving an old and rather decrepit Singer Eight (which he had bought for £15) and headed south. It got him safely to Hawick, luggage and all: 'I chugged my way into the town that afternoon with all my worldly goods and chattels heaped in the back of the aged car.'

When he arrived, the parish priest Father Dan Kelly was in the sitting-room, patiently smoking his clay pipe. It was the Feast of the Assumption of Our Lady and a White Father missionary had been there to help out with the Masses — he rather doubtfully wished me happy days and departed.

Hardly had Gordon sat down than Father Dan's housekeeper came in with a letter for him in the Archbishop's rather indecipherable handwriting. Gordon apologised to Father Dan, and read it.

The Archbishop was writing from Ampleforth, the Benedictine monastery in Yorkshire. He told him that Father Dan had appealed to Rome against his *deposition* (removal) as parish priest. However, Gordon was not to worry and take no cognisance of this.

As they talked, Father Dan gave him a list of parish collections to read out at the Sunday Masses. The next morning Gordon took the list into the pulpit, told the people that he understood he should read it, but that he had been appointed to preach the Gospel. If they wanted to hear their names and contributions called out, he didn't want their collections. If they did not, they wouldn't want him to waste his time and theirs. He preached his homily and followed the same line at the second Mass.

Before the congregation had moved out, he got to the door and was greeted kindly. One man, Hugh Heslin, a joiner in one of the mills, waited patiently and, when most had gone, grasped his hand. 'Father,' he said, 'don't drive us. Just give us a lead and we'll follow you and do whatever you wish.'

'I met my first Hawick friends after my first morning service in Buccleuch Street,' Gordon later reminded the people of Hawick at the 1973 Common Riding, 'and I knew I had come to a town and a people I should never wish to leave.'

Next day Gordon took to the road to start his visitations. He returned depressed. From not one door did he receive a response. It was only later that he realised that there was no one in! The War was on. The men were in the Army. The women were working either in the hosiery or tweed mills or the munitions factory. Soon he learned that only the sick or housebound could be visited by day. To visit the workers you had to go at night.

Life was not easy in those days. Returning in 1973, Gordon (by this time Cardinal Gray) addressed the people of Hawick and spoke of 'those anxious, troubled War years, when there was hardly a home in the town that did not dread the sight of the telegram boy, hardly a home in the town that had not a vacant place at table and a photograph on the mantleshelf of father, son or daughter in uniform.'

There were also lighter moments. Not long after Gordon had arrived, he went to visit a woman in her house. He had been told that she was 'hard up'. In Hawick, that expression meant she was 'not well'. He went to visit the house and, after talking to the woman for some time, he got up to leave. On his way out he put a ten shilling note on the mantlepiece and went away. Naturally, the woman's daughter came running after him to ask what the ten shilling note was for. He tried to explain to her that he had been told that her mother was not in her best financial circumstances. Laughing, the girl soon explained to him what being 'hard up' meant!

In the parish, Hugh Heslin became Father Gordon's right-hand man. He helped him with his boys' club. They turned the old wash-house into a workshop and together they made wooden toys and sold them for charities at Christmas. Heslin worked with him, guiding Gordon as, over 18 months, they made the altar rails out of the best oak.

Gordon soon settled into the community. He was made an ARP warden and became a life member of the Hawick Archaeological Society. A number of his parishioners played rugby for Hawick and their new parish priest became an avid fan of the 'Greens'.

He set up a greenhouse where he grew tomatoes, marrows, peaches and nectarines, and many a cold morning saw him up at five to stoke the anthracite boiler for the church.

Not long afterwards Gordon was appointed Dean of the Borders, at that time being the youngest Dean in Scotland. He loved Hawick and the people took to him. The Woman's Guild flourished. The Girls' Club was kept occupied. Each Christmas a pantomime was performed (written by Father Gray in doggerel verse). Fred Chisholm arranged all the stage effects and scenery. His daughter Peggy chose the songs and also made the costumes.

Poor Father Dan's health broke down, and after a year he was rightly, but perhaps a little unkindly (Gordon felt), retired. He was a sick man and died a year later from cancer of the colon. There followed a succession of curates – Father Watt, Father Eric Gordon and Father Tom Engelen.

The centenary of Hawick parish was celebrated in 1944. Archbishop McDonald offered the Mass with music from the *Mass of St Cecilia*. Bishop George Bennett of Aberdeen, a former parish priest, preached. They all stayed for two nights in the tiny presbytery. Although the War was on, Gordon managed to acquire a bottle of whisky and two bottles of Algerian wine by devious means.

They were difficult, the War years. Beside the parish itself and Stirches Convent, Gordon had to look after Stobs Camp which straddled the Border. He never knew if he was going to be in England or Scotland; it depended on what hut he was sent to – an Italian POW camp south of Newcastleton; or a German POW camp in Hawick where there was a staunch group of Catholics who were eventually allowed to attend the Stobs Camp services. There were also the Ulster Rifles (West Sussex), a mixed battalion of Guards, Irish Guards and Poles.

Never an idle moment, but he loved the people of Hawick, Catholic and non-Catholic alike.

He had discovered in his travels that one of the German POWs was a priest, so Gordon got him a clerical suit and a bike and allowed him to attend to the needs of his fellow-prisoners, some of whom came each Sunday to sing in the church choir, and one of whom played the organ for Mass.

Apart from the Cottage Hospital, the TB Hospital and the Isolation Hospital, Gordon had Stirches Convent as a parish chaplaincy and St Margaret's Convent at which he was the ordinary confessor. And he was a member of Roxburgh Education Committee.

One of the saddest days of Gordon's life was the morning when he received a phone call from Archbishop McDonald asking him to meet him at his parents' house in Eskbank that morning.

He drove up in his little Austin Seven (which his father had bought for him when the brakes failed after a short run in the old Singer). When he got to Eskbank, the Archbishop met him and informed him that he had been appointed by the Scottish Bishops as Rector of Blairs College, the National Junior Seminary, near Aberdeen.

'I saw His Grace yesterday,' he wrote to his housekeeper, Mary Collins, 'and he hinted that I shall be going north about the end of the month. His Grace says as far as the appointment goes, all is in order. No way out apparently and the Bishops are in agreement. The Edinburgh clergy, from yesterday's reception, seem solidly behind me and I've no doubt the rest will co-operate once I'm up there.'

It was only the day before, the eighth Sunday after Pentecost, that Gordon had preached on the text 'Render an account of thy stewardship, for now thou canst be steward no longer'.

'It was the last thing he wanted,' recalls his curate at the time, Father Thomas Engelen, 'to be taken away from the pastoral work he loved. He spent extra time in prayer, asking the Good Lord to allow something to happen so that the appointment would be cancelled. However, as nothing did happen, he accepted the appointment as God's will for him.'

Gordon had never seen Blairs College before, but he was given orders to report there on 15th August 1944, four years to the day since he had come to Hawick.

'My only consolation,' observed Cardinal Gray looking back, 'comes from the wise advice of my old seminary Rector, Monsignor Mallett: "Do what you are told. If it works out you can be happy. If it does not you can still be happy because it was not what you chose but what you were *told* to do. Obedience is better than sacrifice".'

With these words in mind, he moved out of Hawick, leaving behind him, in the mind of at least one parishioner, the memory of being 'the priest who kept chickens'.

CHAPTER 4

Blairs College

FATHER Gordon left Hawick with a heavy heart, his little Austin Seven filled to capacity with such personal belongings as he thought he might require. His instructions were to take over as Rector for the beginning of the new session towards the end of August.

However, at the last moment he received a phone call from Archbishop McDonald intimating that there were problems at Blairs and that he should await further word from him.

Consequently he went home to Eskbank and, as the weeks passed by, had the longest holiday he had enjoyed during his whole life as a priest.

The previous Rector, Monsignor McGonagle, who had given long years to Blairs as Professor and Rector, had been 'retired' by the bishops, and the College staff were on the point of mass resignation. Eventually (sometime around 14th October), Gordon drove up to the College (which he had never visited before in his life).

'I remember well the shock I had,' the Cardinal remembered, 'when, about six in the evening, I gazed on the massive complex of granite buildings that was Blairs! I had expected a smallish College such as I had known at Mark Cross, and not this imposing and splendid building crowned with the Papal tiara and rising stately and high with the needle spire of the College Chapel.'

He drew up at the steps to the main entrance. A priest in cassock, eyes cast down on the prayers in his breviary (prayer book), came up to the car. 'Father Gray, I presume? I shall take you to your room.' So, silently, the two men walked up the stairs, along the length of the corridor and arrived at Gordon's bedroom opposite his sitting-room. 'Benediction is at 7.30, followed by supper.' And he left Gordon who was a little depressed at the cool, if not frigid, welcome.

In due course he heard the sound of many footsteps and followed their direction. He arrived in the sacristy – very much a stranger in a strange (and not, apparently, very friendly) land.

However, he suddenly received a slap on the back – his first big break – and a big, smiling face and a warm, welcoming voice boomed out: 'Great to see you, Gordon. Happy days. I'm Father Steve McGill.' He took Gordon to the choir stall and, after Benediction, to a chair in the dining-room. In came Archbishop McDonald and Archbishop Campbell who had apparently arrived to install Gordon as Rector, procurator and headmaster all rolled into one.

Gordon was relieved when the meal was over and the two Archbishops with the acting Rector made their way to his sitting-room for a dram. Gordon sipped a sherry, not yet having been introduced to the therapeutic value of Glenlivet!

Arrangements were made for altars and times of Masses and for his formal introduction to the staff, and installation at 10 o'clock next day. Gordon was glad when the festivities came to an end and he was able to get into bed.

Next morning they assembled in the Queen Mary room. It was all very formal. A chair and a *prie-dieu* (kneeling stool) were provided for Gordon. He knelt down, made his profession of faith and took the oath against Modernism. Then, exhortations from the Archbishops and Bishop Bennett. The formal meeting ended. The professors went back to their classes. Then the Archbishop took the new Rector for a walk and told him that, when he had got a grip on the running of the college, the Bishops would give him the help of a procurator and headmaster.

The first days and weeks were a period of finding out, going through cupboards, looking through account books, wondering where his duties and responsibilities began and ended. The only consolation came when, after lunch, the Bishops left.

Then Father James Kilpatrick made a pronouncement: 'Now that the top brass have gone at last, welcome Gordon and we'll all back you up. We'll meet in the billiard-room after supper for a *festa* [party].' It was a good *festa* – Father Frank Duffy played the piano and the boys in the dormitories above almost certainly lost a good deal of their beauty sleep as the heavens resounded with songs in an atmosphere of relaxation and peace.

Gordon had much to learn. The Blairs estate extended to over 1,500 acres. There were two home farms – one at Blairs and another along the road at Kintalene, which had recently been modernised and housed a dozen attested Ayrshire cows under the care of a grieve, two farm-workers and a dairy-maid.

The Blairs farm was similarly staffed and housed perhaps 20 Irish cows and an Aberdeen Angus bull. In those days a bull calf could fetch £5. The cows supplied the College with milk adequate to their needs.

The rest of the estate was either planted in forestry or rented as small crofts or houses. In all there were approximately twelve employees. Gordon had never seen PAYE cards before. They had to be sent in regularly – and food tokens, clothing tokens, catering returns, claims for sugar for jam-making, transfer of livestock. There were always forms and statistics for returns.

The College was in the process of being re-wired in preparation for the introduction of 'The Grid'. Previously Blairs had operated on 110 volts generated from the two diesel engines and a roomful of batteries. Work was slow, very slow. Floors went up. Work came to a halt through lack of materials. The contractors complained. The General Electric Company, whom Gordon had contacted personally, blamed the delay on the contractors who, they said, did not pay their bills. The College suffered. The re-wiring eventually extended to over three years!

New houses were in the process of being built, new homes for the college's employees. Two were complete, six at a standstill because they had no water supply. Two of the farm-workers claimed to be 'dowsers', able to find water underground. Gordon used their gifts and dug wells.

He loved that phase of the work – inserting the gelignite in the deep hole that had been dug, attaching the detonator and wires, starting the current, and watching for the results!

The houses were put into use years before the promised county water-supply from a man-made reservoir up the hill at

Clochandighter was completed. However, although the estate and the farm both interested Gordon greatly, and took up a lot of his time – together with the accounts and the never-ending paperwork – his primary responsibility was to care for the staff and the Sisters of St Joseph of Annecy, and the boys.

On news of Gordon's appointment, Bishop George Bennett of Aberdeen had said to him, 'Remember that a seminary is a place where our future priests learn priestly virtue from the example of priests' – advice which Gordon took to heart.

The custom had grown up that 4th and 5th year students should meet in the Oratory for morning prayer, meditation and Mass. The junior boys met in the College chapel where they were given a spiritual talk every morning by Father McGill.

Shortly after he arrived, Gordon joined the senior boys for all the morning spiritual exercises. A few weeks later, after a meeting, some of the staff joined him. Later, he shared with Father McGill the giving of talks to the juniors and he replaced Gordon in the oratory.

The priests on the staff were good, hard-working men. They were a very happy and united community. Gordon had never before met such unity and camaraderie in any religious house.

They met regularly to assess the boys and discuss the problems. There were frank and open meetings, although disagreements on policies were frequent. But always the same conclusion towards their Rector: 'You're the boss. Whatever you decide, we'll back you up.' And they did.

At that time no one on the staff had a teacher's diploma, only two or three had degrees in the subjects they taught. But they worked hard to a very heavy class programme, augmented by extra-classroom activities – housemasters, confessors; sports and recreation.

Despite the pressures and the large numbers of their classes – with around 200 boys and a staff of only twelve teachers – they achieved outstanding results in the Higher Leaving Certificate examinations. There was a narrow range of subjects, but none the worse for that. Maths was the weakest and Science was only a secondary subject during a boy's first two years at College.

After a year, Gordon altered the timetable, thereby imposing an even heavier teaching load on the staff. It was so modified that a boy could follow individual classes according to his ability. So a boy who had come to Blairs after two years in a secondary school, but had studied, for example, neither Latin nor Greek, could do first year in these subjects and third year in the rest.

And so with any subject. By the time the Highers arrived, he was fit for Lowers in the subjects in which he had started late, and for Highers in the rest. It was complicated time-tabling since the staff was numerically small, but it worked well.

Gordon found it difficult to delegate duties. But at Blairs, it was less of a problem. Father McGill, as spiritual director, met each boy regularly; the form masters knew the boys in the form and Father Daniel Boyle, as prefect of discipline, knew them all. And, of course, the professors knew the boys in their classes. Gordon was brought in only in times of crisis when a 'big gun' was needed, or when it was judged best that a boy should be sent home.

For the boys there were no home comforts, no sweets, no pocket money (except when the sweet shop was open). Visits to Aberdeen were restricted to the dentist or hospital. Although the College was closed for a Christmas holiday, the new term, from early January to the end of June, was long. From January to Easter life was pretty hard, and during those months the boys became unsettled and a number gave up and went home.

Gordon came to love Blairs – every stone, every blade of grass. He tried to improve the meals and to introduce a supper more interesting than bread and jam, a repetition of breakfast and tea.

With old John Rae, a great and faithful servant of the college who did all the joinery work and looked after the saw-mill, Gordon built hen-houses. He bought day-old chicks at the market and soon had over 200 laying hens, in addition to geese, ducks and turkeys.

Soon the boys had an egg with their supper. Eaten with relish for a few nights, before they had to go back to bread, jam and more jam. With great difficulty their Rector scrounged under-the-counter, coupon-free tinned meat. It was a great success for two or three nights, and then back to more bread and jam.

Gordon grew an acre of carrots, as much of cabbages, and then tried to vary the diet. But the cabbages became a Christmas pantomime gimmick and the carrots were often left-overs.

'The boys wanted dried peas and dried beans which they lapped up and a most indigestible bread pudding, lovingly known as "Friday pud".'

Boys are very traditional. How Gordon wished he could give them fish and chips. They would have canonised him on the spot! Strange to relate, despite the completely unbalanced diet, the health record was good.

There were the ordinary problems and crises with the boys – fractures and appendicitis, colds and flu and the rest. But it was a disciplined life and they appeared to enjoy and benefit greatly from their training.

The output for senior colleges was good – over 30 per cent of the 'starters' became priests. The Church did not lose the 70 per cent who were left. Throughout Scotland you can find doctors, dentists, head teachers, lawyers, police inspectors and members of Parliament who were Blairs boys, many of whom are now in the forefront of post-Vatican II renewal programmes. Blairs produced rich dividends, if not in priests, at least in dedicated church workers.

Writing to his former housekeeper, Mary Collins, in December 1949, Gordon spoke of his hopes of buying another secondhand car, the brakes of his present machine being 'quite useless, and in my advancing years I think I need something safer. Probably the next will be about 1920 vintage. Candidly, I am sorely tempted to get a pony and trap. It would be slower perhaps, and just a little conspicuous, but there would be no petrol problem!'

The year 1950 proved to be a time of great personal loss for Gordon, removing two of the pillars of his life – one deeply personal, the other related to his chosen vocation. On 19th April 1950 his father died, a time of profound grief. A month later, on 22nd May, Archbishop McDonald passed away. When the news came, Gordon wept once again.

'He was,' said Gordon Joseph of Archbishop McDonald later, 'a man loved and admired by many, but feared and unloved by others.' A great leader, but with a most unassuming manner, McDonald was not afraid to enter the political arena, and his attacks on Communism earned him the displeasure of the Government and Parliament. During the attacks of Protestant Action, he held back his Catholic flock from taking any retaliatory measures. However, he did not endear himself to his clergy by his virtual ban on their owning cars or going to the theatre or cinema.

Gordon had a tremendous admiration for the Archbishop – his drive, his oratory and his friendship. Gordon knew that – like most enthusiasts – the Archbishop had sometimes been a poor judge of character and of the abilities of those whose views did not coincide with his own. For him people had been either black or white. Gordon knew he could be precipitate and rash in his decisions. But, he was an outstanding Archbishop. He had simple faith. He was a deeply spiritual priest. He was, for Gordon at least, an inspiration.

Although on occasions Gordon had disagreed with the Archbishop, he listened to Gordon patiently. Little did Gordon know that, years before his death, he had declared to his trusted friends that Gordon would succeed him as Archbishop of St Andrews and Edinburgh.

Archbishop McDonald's body was brought back to St Bennet's to lie in an open coffin in the chapel dressed in his episcopal vestments. On the following day at St Mary's Cathedral, the panegyric was preached by his old adversary, Archbishop Campbell of Glasgow.

At Blairs life went on, and so did the weeks and months after the Archbishop's death. Occasionally, names of a possible successor were raised and discussed at meals by members of the staff. Monsignor Clapperton? Bishop James Scanlan? Father Tyndal Atkinson? A year passed. Then, Father Gordon Joseph Gray's name was mentioned and, as the next month arrived, more frequently.

On 20th June Gordon was doing a bit of painter work in a small annexe to his bedroom, with the intention of inserting a toilet and wash-hand basin. Around half past three Sister Christine knocked and came in to find him in a boiler suit covered in paint. She had the afternoon post and said, 'Here is a letter from the Apostolic Delegate.'

Gordon replied, 'Leave it on the bed, please Sister. It will be about National Service.'

Gordon Joseph finished his painting for the day, cleaned up and washed. Then he went into the sitting-room and opened the post.

The letter from the Delegate was not about military service, but a personal letter from Archbishop Godfrey to the effect that the *Holy Father* (Pius XII) had appointed him as Archbishop of St Andrews and Edinburgh and that the announcement would be published on 28th June if he accepted.

Then, 'if you accept, please send immediately a reply in the following words ... ', and he gave a coded message for his reply, ending his letter with the words *Spiritus Sanctus Subveniet* (the Holy Spirit will help), words later used by Gordon for his motto as Archbishop.

When Gordon had revived, he went along to the dining-room for tea, inwardly in a mental turmoil, yet canonically *sub secreto Sancti Officio* – bound to silence. There was no optional message to send if he had wished to refuse. The *Sanctus Spiritus Subveniet* was his only anchor.

After tea, he was due to go with Father Kilpatrick and Father Duffy to Cruden Bay to visit a site for the boys' day out. He told Father Kilpatrick that he didn't want to drive and that he had to go to Aberdeen General Post Office with letters and suchlike.

He agreed to drive Gordon's old jalopy. They visited the chosen location, agreed that it was suitable and drove back to Blairs, himself agonising with the secret he could not mention until noon on 28th June.

On 28th June, Father Steve McGill was to set off for America. They all had a farewell *festa* the evening before. In the morning Gordon saw him off on his train, without being able to divulge the news that would break at noon.

Father Hugh McGurk was waiting for Gordon when he returned. He ambled along, tactfully asking leading questions. Father Willie McLaughlin of St Columba's, Edinburgh phoned, asking for news of the appointment. Scrupulously, Gordon said, 'I know nothing.'

Little did he know that on the evening of 27th June, Vatican Radio had announced his appointment; Father McGurk's father had heard the news and phoned him, and Father McLaughlin had also been told by a parishioner who had heard Vatican Radio.

A little boy came into Gordon's room about quarter to twelve to report that he had broken cups, saucers and plates! Gordon told him to see Father Kilpatrick and to ask him to come and see the Rector. But the culprit wanted an answer at once to his confession in order to put him out of his misery. Gordon let him go with a telling-off.

Some minutes later, just before noon, Father Kilpatrick arrived. He looked at Gordon and said: 'God help us, have we to train another Rector still wet behind the ears? Let's have a dram.' So he summoned the staff and, as they arrived, the phone rang – it was Bishop Scanlan (then coadjutor for the diocese of Dunkeld) sending his congratulations.

Suddenly, someone remembered that there were boys due to sit an exam on Christian Doctrine. In a relieved mood, Gordon cancelled the exam and one of the staff told the boys the news. Sounds of merriment resounded through Blairs. It would mean an extra holiday!

That Friday everyone was late for lunch. The menu was boiled cod and the phone kept ringing.

The staff and the boys left for their holiday a couple of days later. It was a relief for the new Archbishop. He wanted peace and quiet to think and there was as usual so much for the Rector to do when the session came to an end.

There were many interruptions. Many visitors, never-ending phone calls, a mountain of post. The account books for the annual audit had to be brought up to date for the end of the financial year (the end of July); parents of new boys accepted for the new session had to be notified and given such information as was required – health reports, college outfits needed; date for opening; train times *etc, etc*. The usual tradesmen required for maintenance of buildings had to be seen and directed as to what was necessary. The routine work for the estate and farm had to go on.

Bishop Scanlan phoned to say he would like to come for a break at Blairs for a couple of weeks. Gordon was glad. He was always a loyal friend to him. His urbanity made him the most welcome guest in polite society since the days of the late eighteenth century Bishop John Geddes. Years later, preaching Archbishop Scanlan's panegyric in 1976, Gordon would describe him as 'the last of the prince-bishops'.

Gordon was sure he would have loved to have been appointed to Edinburgh, but Rome had decided, and how well and loyally he backed the new Archbishop up.

For Gordon, Bishop Scanlan had one fault during those summer weeks of 1951 – he ate so slowly! Gordon was up to the eyes in work, but lunch regularly merged into tea-time.

Father Steve McGill was appointed to succeed Gordon as Rector. When he returned from America at the beginning of August, Gordon Joseph handed over to him, after giving him some driving-lessons in the football field.

About the middle of the month Gordon said goodbye to his beloved Blairs with its joys and sorrows, its good days and bad.

CHAPTER 5

St Bennet's

IN the early evening of 15th August 1951, Archbishop-elect Gordon Gray, driving his ancient (but once luxurious) Triumph Dolomite, arrived at his new home in a secluded corner of Edinburgh's Greenhill Gardens.

As he got out of the car at St Bennet's, he was met by Sister Zita and Sister Philomena who had been caretaking during the interregnum of 15 months. Also there to meet him was Mac, a Kerry Blue – the dog who came by day, returned home to his owner at night, and hated the sight of Gordon as an intruder. They never made friends, despite blandishments and chocolates.

Gordon was as wise as Solomon and never asked the Provincial of the Ursulines of Jesus if she would leave the Sisters to look after the house and himself. She never contacted him and he took it for granted.

The garden of Archbishop's House at St Bennet's was unkempt and wild. When the War broke out, the back had been planted with fruit trees enclosed within a six-foot high fence surmounted by barbed wire. It came close on six feet from the windows.

The house itself had been the official residence of Archbishops of St Andrews and Edinburgh since 1890. In Scottish Baronial style, it has a small Byzantine chapel attached to it, whose green domed copper roofs and cruciform construction in snecked rubble is a familiar, if exotic, local landmark.

But in 1951 the house was cold, sparsely furnished and its interior walls distempered, with the exception of the dining-room and staircase, which had been papered. There was no central heating in operation and the wall-paper flapped with every draught.

The archiepiscopal car – a 1934 Austin limousine – was in the garage, shining and polished as it always was under John Pinkman's careful eye. That, and driving the Archbishop, was then his full-time job. In return he had a free house and two pounds and five shillings a week.

Gordon soon decided he preferred to stay in a small manageable house. Early on he realised he could not move – the historic value of the chapel (built by the Marquess of Bute) would be an insuperable obstacle to the sale of the property. He decided to start with the garden, and, by degrees, turn the house into a home.

He had a good night's sleep and, in the morning, offered Holy Mass and arranged to see 71-year old Monsignor Chase, his old parish priest, friend and, until his appointment as Archbishop, vicar capitular (temporary senior administrator). Gordon immediately appointed him vicar general in place of 46-year old Monsignor Breen with whom he felt he could not work productively. He was a fine priest, one of Archbishop McDonald's Cambridge-educated elite, but in his personal relations with Gordon he had always been distant and unhelpful and would not make the running of the archdiocese easy.

Gordon took *Spiritus Sanctus Subveniet* (The Holy Spirit will help) as the motto of his coat of arms. He was now responsible for a large diocese, stretching from Fife in the North to the Borders, and from Dunbar in the East to Kilsyth in the West – a total area of some 30,000 square kilometres. There were over 100 parishes, 80 schools and 30 to 40 religious houses to visit.

The Feast of St Matthew, 21st September, was agreed upon as the date for Gordon's episcopal consecration in the perpendicular Gothic of St Mary's Cathedral at Broughton Place, with its commanding position at the top of Leith Walk.

Archbishop William Godfrey, then Apostolic Delegate, found that date convenient. For personal reasons Gordon wanted him as principal celebrant at the Mass. He wanted to be in the apostolic line from Pope St Pius X.

Gordon had little to do with the arrangements. He met the Chapter of Canons in the Cathedral as the Code of Canon Law prescribed, presented his Bull of Appointment and officially took over the administration.

The hard work of invitations, luncheons, arrival of guests, departures, accommodation, was left to Father James Monaghan, Father Patrick Grady and Canon James Turner. There were a number of refusals. To the invitation to the Moderator, or a representative of the Church of Scotland, came a blunt refusal.

Representation at church services had always been a problem between denominations – in 1902, for example, the Catholic Church had felt itself unable to send bishops to the Coronation at Westminster; while as late as 1965 the Scottish Catholic Hierarchy still forbade Catholic guiders and guides to take part in inter-denominational services or prayers held in non-Catholic churches.

The Archbishop-to-be spent a week in retreat at Sancta Maria Abbey, Nunraw under the spiritual care of Father Ambrose. He had his tonsure cut by a Brother (who was a very novice barber!) and came home.

Archbishop Godfrey and his secretary, Father Cashman (later Bishop Cashman of Arundel), was driving north in a Rolls Royce. It broke down near Newcastle. Gordon waited impatiently – he had to fast before his consecration. The supper was ruined and poor Sister Zita agonised.

The following morning, their magnificent vestments of gold, purple and black flashing in the September sun, two processions made their way from Cathedral House in York Place to the Cathedral – the archbishops and bishops on the one hand, and on the other, the canons of the Chapter.

Present in the Cathedral for the three-hour long service were the Lord Advocate, Mr John Wheatley KC, MP, members of the diplomatic corps, the Duke of Norfolk, the Marquess of Lothian, Major Michael Crichton-Stuart, Lord Carmont and Sir Hew Hamilton-Dalrymple.

Among the clergy present were Archbishop Donald Campbell of Glasgow, Bishop Grey Graham (formerly of St Andrews and Edinburgh), Bishop Kenneth Grant of Argyll and the Isles, and Bishop James Black of Paisley. Representing the English Hierarchy were the Bishops of Hexham and Newcastle, and the Bishop of Lancaster. Others included the Abbot of Fort Augustus, Dom Wulstan Knowles; the Abbot of Nunraw, Columban Mulcahy; and the Prior of Pluscarden Abbey, Dom Norbert Cowin. The proudest person present was, of course, the new Archbishop's mother.

Following the public examination of the Archbishop-elect as to his orthodoxy in faith and morals, he prostrated himself before the altar. Then came the laying-on of hands, the Consecration prayer, the anointing, the presentation of gloves and ring, then the mitre, then the pastoral staff. Finally, the enthronement. During the offertory, six members of religious Orders approached from the centre aisle, carrying two lighted wax candles, two loaves and two small barrels of wine.

After the vesting and enthronement, the choir sang the *Te Deum* and the new Archbishop came down the steps from the sanctuary to bless the congregation, beginning with his mother and his family.

Great enthusiasm greeted him at the Cathedral door when the ceremony ended, and at the North British Hotel where there followed a celebratory lunch. At the hotel other guests joined the party – the Lord Provost, James Miller; the Right Revd Kenneth Warner, Episcopal Bishop of Edinburgh; the Revd Nevile David-son of Glasgow Cathedral and the Chief Rabbi of Scotland, Isaac Cohen.

Gordon, in his address, thanked God that his mother had been present at the ceremony in the church and said he was sure his father was watching: 'My first thanks under God, must be to my parents. My mother, thank God, is present this morning; my father, not spared to be present, is, I know, watching.'

The episcopate, he added, had brought him home again to Edinburgh. 'Mine is no easy task. Our late Archbishop was great as a man, with vision and foresight. He had electric energy and could sweep a horizon, yet note the smallest detail.'

Eventually, after a meal that included Liebfraumilch Blue Nun to drink and pears *à la Cardinal* as a sweet, all the guests left and Archbishop Gordon Joseph Gray returned home to St Bennet's with Archbishop Godfrey. Next morning he took the latter to the railway station, returned home and found himself, as he was to put it, 'for the first time as a bishop, alone and a little bewildered.'

He didn't know where to begin. Archbishop McDonald had

the custom of confirming in parishes every three years. In 1949 his health had been indifferent. In 1950, just prior to his death, he had had to opt out of all public engagements. Consequently, there were heavy arrears in Confirmation ceremonies. So Gordon Joseph asked his clergy for information and found that he could fill his days visiting parishes and confirming for many, many months.

He made up his programme – two parishes each Sunday and every week day evening. It was hard, but he was young and, in those days of mass rallies, a new Archbishop was a novelty. He was asked to visit, preach and give talks throughout the country and even south of the Border. Little wonder that, at the end of his first year, his voice was on the point of fading out!

But it was a productive year that satisfied him. A year of cease-less activity, of meeting people and of far too little time for prayer – except for his Breviary and evening Rosary in the chapel at St Bennet's.

Very gradually, at first through Mr Van de Rydt (the Consul General for the Netherlands who invited him to his house to a reception for consuls), he began to receive invitations from many quarters to attend functions – from the Army, the Law Society of Scotland, the BBC.

Gordon Joseph did not enjoy them greatly, but he felt they were an acknowledgment that the Catholic Church existed and was of importance. The invitations became more frequent and escalated to such a degree that eventually he was compelled to select those which he felt to be most useful. In fact, he found later that his name was on the official St Andrew's House list.

Fortunately, the circle of 'regulars' at such receptions was com-paratively small and soon he got to know most of the guests and could introduce strangers to others.

Receptions were time-consuming to Gordon Joseph, and indeed boring. But they gave him the opportunity of becoming known and meeting people socially whose help and intervention could frequently be called upon when support on some problem was required.

'I remember coming home from one such function,' said the Cardinal, 'in the company of Monsignor Patrick Quille, whose charm, wit and friendly manner did so much to gain entry to areas of public life in the past closed to Catholics. "Your Grace," he said, for we had hardly met all evening, "I think that, after tonight, you must have realised the value of your Apostolate of Cocktail Parties!'"

But there were other nights when the new Archbishop would turn into the drive of St Bennet's after a particularly arduous function, put away his car in the garage and enter the house. As he put on the lights, he would see the stern portraits of his predecessors staring down at him with disapproval, and he would slink past them up to bed.

In many ways being a Rector of Blairs was the traditional method of grooming future bishops. Unlike a parish appointment, the Rector had responsibility for a team of up to 20 priests; he had to oversee the management of a large property; he had to care for 200 boys and for farm-staff; and he also got to know all the Scottish Bishops as he played host twice a year to the residential bishops' conference.

Having said that, the duties of an archbishop would have presented Gordon Joseph with unfamiliar challenges. He now had responsibility for some 200 priests; he had jurisdiction over a very far-flung diocese; he had to keep himself up to date in preaching and teaching; and keep the diocese financially viable with respect to churches, halls and religious houses. And, although he was able to consult others in taking decisions, he was at times acutely aware that the ultimate responsibility for all these matters was his.

From his predecessor, Andrew Joseph McDonald, he inherited a diocesan machine that was deftly-organised in financial terms. The former had become Archbishop in 1929, and found an organisational shambles. He proceeded to shake up the local church organisation. One way of doing this was to invite many religious Orders to establish themselves in the diocese. But he left behind a relationship with priests and people that was in some ways uneasy and untrusting.

A man of vision, with a ruthlessly logical turn of mind, Archbishop McDonald nevertheless had caused some antagonism. His policy of choosing some men to send to Oxford or Cambridge was far-sighted in one respect. It brought in men trained particularly in the Social Sciences, which Archbishop McDonald considered essential for the combating of Communism. But this policy did sometimes cause difficulties when they returned to Scotland, in that there was often no structure into which their specialised educational qualifications could be fitted.

In addition, he sometimes strained relations between himself and his parish clergy with his practice of appearing unannounced at parish services. Father Reginald Hodgson, his secretary from 1940-1950, recalls the occasion when the Archbishop had heard that some of his priests were not starting Mass on time.

'He asked his chauffeur to drive him to a particular church and arranged the time of his arrival to coincide with the beginning of Mass – the time advertised in the directory.

'Arriving at the church, the Archbishop went in and sat at the back. There was no sign of the priest at the altar. Someone in the congregation recognised him and ran to tell the parish priest. He, poor man, suspecting nothing, went down to ask his Grace if he wanted anything. "Yes," was the terse reply, "I want to see you start Mass on time." Needless to say, when he went on such campaigns, the telephone wires between presbyteries were red hot!

Austere monk that he was, endowed with tremendous physical energy, Archbishop McDonald had swum Loch Ness in his early days and replicated the 40-mile route taken by Montrose's army before the battle of Inverlochy. Archbishop McDonald was not averse to ascetic habits. He was said, when returning home late from outwith Edinburgh, to have spent the night on a bench at Waverley Station in order not to disturb the sleep of the Sisters who acted as his housekeepers at St Bennet's.

During the incumbency of Archbishop McDonald, clerical life had been strictly regulated in today's terms – priests were required to wear a long clerical jacket which reached to the tips of their fingers, and they were allowed to own a motor car only with the Archbishop's permission, and visits to the cinema were banned!

In his zeal to establish efficiency, he seems to have disapproved of long-standing friendships among the clergy, particularly where priests in neighbouring parishes met regularly to enjoy innocent recreations such as golf or cards.

Finally, the new Archbishop inherited some unprovoked residual resentments of long standing, produced, for example, by the accidental loss in 1934 of enormous revenues from the estate of Canon John Gray (no relation), parish priest of St Peter's in Morningside. His fortune (inherited from the Russian émigré André Raffalovitch) was accidentally left, not partly to the archdiocese as he had originally intended, but entirely to the Dominican house in the city – in spite of the Dominicans' efforts to secure a more equitable distribution of the funds.

Then there was the familiar East-West divide in the Catholic Church, continued by Leo XIII in his apostolic letter *Ex supremo* of 1878, with the re-creation of two archdioceses in the South of Scotland, which echoed other spheres of national secular life.

Coming, as he did, from a laird's family, knowing no Gaelic, Archbishop McDonald represented a very different cultural strain to Archbishop Campbell of Glasgow – who was unaristocratic and Gaelic-speaking, with English as a second language. The mutual distrust of McDonalds for Campbells, after all, reached back to the Glencoe Massacre.

According to Archbishop Gordon Gray in later years, it was only with the advent (1964-74) of his friend, the cultivated Archbishop James Scanlan, that the rift between East and West began to heal. Like Gordon Gray, James Scanlan had been educated in the south (at St Edmund's, Ware and at the Military College, Sandhurst). He had returned to Scotland with a sophisticated breadth of learning:

'His Glasgow birth, education and law degrees,' wrote Gordon Gray, 'his charm and gentlemanly manner, his conversation and personal knowledge of everyone in the public gaze, completely changed the public image of Catholic Glasgow which had been seen as simply Irish in outlook (and Catholic through loyalty to the Celtic Football Club). He gave it a new dimension by transforming it into a church that really mattered, a church with a voice that commanded a listening ear and respect.'

The new Archbishop's primary long-term task was, therefore, to try to heal similar underlying relational disparities at home. He set about doing so with great vigour, but without the benefit of a clear model for delegating responsibilities. At this time wartime government restrictions on building had just been relaxed and Archbishop Gray was besieged with requests for new church building programmes. All these factors, including the great back-log of confirmations – on 28th September 1952 he confirmed 394 children at St Mary's, Stirling – led, after around 18 months, to a breakdown in his health, to complete physical and mental exhaustion, from which he would only slowly recover.

For the time being, life in the universal Church went on much as before. The Catholic Church worldwide was reasonably satisfied with the old ways, complacent perhaps, but, to a bishop, offering few problems and no confrontations.

There was little important internal dialogue, little that seemed to require discussion. Priests were moved in and out of parishes and they accepted such moves without the need for consultation. The attitude of the clergy was simply that of obedience to the bishop – 'He's the boss. I'll go where I'm sent. If it works, good. If it doesn't, it's the bishop's mistake, not mine!' And here was the root cause of Archbishop Gray's soul-searching.

The everyday work of a bishop not only involved a wide range of meetings or functions – secular as well as religious – but each bishop feels the need to make time for prayer. This is often extremely difficult, apart from early in the morning or late at night. At St Bennet's, the adjacent chapel made it possible to relax in prayer.

The planned routine of a bishop's day would often be broken by unexpected calls from heads of religious communities, or by visiting dignitaries, or by parish clergy wishing to speak to the bishop alone. Of all a bishop's responsibilities, time with his priests would be most important – whether dealing with humdrum matters or with urgent personal or parish affairs.

One of Archbishop Gray's first problems on coming to the diocese was to regularise the sad situation of the Poor Clares' Convent at Mount Alvernia in Edinburgh.

Some years before, during the time of Archbishop McDonald, a minor religious 'schism' had arisen in the monastery. The *Extern* Sisters were led by a very independent Sister – Edith – who apparently would not accept the authority of the Abbess of the *Intern* Sisters who lived inside the Enclosure.

Eventually the crisis came to a head and the Archbishop closed the convent, dispersed the Interns to other Poor Clare Houses and, finally, placed an *interdict* (local ban) on the Extern Sisters who had refused to move.

The latter, however, had many friends – among them Doull Connolly, a lawyer. Archbishop McDonald took the Externs to court in order to evict them, since the property belonged to the trustees of the diocese.

He lost the case – which naturally hit the headlines and was given great publicity in the Press. Although excommunicated, friends of the Externs provided transport for them so that two or three times a week they could go to Glasgow and, with the Archbishop of Glasgow's permission, they received the Sacraments in his diocese. Canonically, he was no doubt correct, since they had become excommunicated only so far as the Archdiocese of St Andrews and Edinburgh was concerned.

Gordon Joseph was determined to clear up the scandal and was working strenuously to do so, but quietly. Sister Edith, however, had friends in the Congregation of Religious in Rome, and, as a result, he received a letter ordering him to lift the excommunication and to let the Sisters remain in peace in the convent premises.

He was very angry, since such a procedure undermined his negotiations to reopen the monastery with a new Intern community from England. Gordon Joseph contacted the Apostolic Delegate, Archbishop Godfrey, to the effect that such interference from the Congregation of Religious in the work of a local bishop left him with no option but to resign as Ordinary.

Archbishop Godfrey at once replied and told him not to worry and that he would contact the Congregation of Religious. What he said or wrote, Gordon Joseph never knew, but thereafter he was left to solve his problem without further interference.

Eventually, when the Intern quarters had been renovated and the dry rot eradicated, the new community joyfully took possession. They had agreed with his conditions. The two leaders of the Externs were offered the opportunity of entering as Interns, and the remaining Sisters were found places in Poor Clare Convents in England where everyone settled happily and gratefully.

During the time of the Cardinal's retirement, the Poor Clare Sisters themselves decided to disperse from their monastery at Liberton, Edinburgh, moving to other different communities.

But the Poor Clares had one important and continuing link with Edinburgh. As Archbishop, Gordon Joseph had many varied responsibilities. One of these was to preside as a judge over the cause of any individual whom the Catholic community believed to be a saint.

In 1931 Archbishop McDonald had gathered the evidence for the case of Margaret Sinclair, an ordinary working girl from Edinburgh who had been, among other things, a French polisher and trade union member, before becoming a Poor Clare nun. She died, after a long and painful illness, in 1925.

Margaret's writings were examined in Rome and approved in 1939. In February 1942 Pope Pius XII ratified the solemn introduction of her cause. Ten years later an Apostolic Process in the Cause of Beatification was begun at St Mary's Cathedral. Archbishop Gray and four other judges took part in the inquiry and a French Franciscan from Rome, Father Brisebois, was also present as Promoter of the Faith (*Devil's Advocate*), whose job it was to find objections to beatification.

The court sat daily for several weeks, during which witnesses were examined. In October 1952 the Process was closed at St Patrick's Church in the Cowgate, where Margaret Sinclair was baptised, received her First Holy Communion and Confirmation, and where parishioners who knew her still worshipped.

Cardinal William Heard, who was based in Rome but was himself a native of Edinburgh and, like Margaret Sinclair's father, a convert to the Catholic faith, approached the Congregation of Rites in Rome. He then informed Monsignor John McQuillan of Troon, the vice-postulator of the cause of Margaret Sinclair, of these moves.

The Archbishop commented: 'I am very glad that Cardinal Heard has given this information to Monsignor McQuillan.'

One of the most pressing problems for the Archbishop was to foresee the needs of the expanding diocese. It was clear to Gordon Joseph that the demolition of appallingly bad slum properties, and their replacement by modern housing outwith the old city and town boundaries, would necessitate the building of new churches and the foundation of new parishes.

The Union of Catholic Mothers had been given the task of praying for vocations (to the priesthood and the religious life) by Archbishop McDonald as a way of highlighting the problem to lay people.

In his last two years as Rector of Blairs, Gordon Joseph had found it necessary to limit the number of boys who wished to enter the college. Each diocese was given a quota. He had converted the college sick-bay into an open dormitory for the first year boys. The number of students who had to be placed in the senior seminaries had increased. The Rector had the task of finding necessary places to receive them. By 1950 the position had become impossible. With the War years over and military service at an end, many students returned from the Forces, intent on continuing their training for the priesthood.

Accommodation for students left much to be desired – St Peter's, Bearsden had been destroyed by fire in the course of work to eradicate dry rot, and students from the Western dioceses had to be placed at large houses in Cardross and Kilmahew which had been purchased by the Archbishop of Glasgow. Neither St Edmund's, Ware nor Oscott could take Scottish senior students any longer.

On the Continent, the Scots College in Valladolid, Spain was closed as a result of the Spanish Civil War, and accommodation at the Scots College in Rome was quite inadequate for national needs. Although the Scottish Bishops had the right to places in France – at Issy and Coutances – only students who had a reasonable grasp of French could usefully be sent there. The upshot was that Archbishop Gordon Joseph realised that Scots must provide for their own needs by founding their own senior seminary.

Before the Second Vatican Council (1960) the tradition in many countries had been to locate seminaries in rural areas, far from the crowded centres of population. After all, seminaries were places for prayer, study and spiritual formation – there was little consideration of pastoral experience at that time.

When he was parish priest in Hawick and needed to come up to Edinburgh, Gordon Joseph frequently took the route via Soutra

Hill, the ancient gateway to Scotland used by pilgrims and marauding armies alike.

Nestling below the road, two or three miles north of St Boswells, stood a large, baronial mansion house in red stone, set in rather overgrown lawns, surrounded by a sea of rhododendrons.

On a number of occasions Gordon Joseph had stopped and thought what a wonderful building it would make for a senior seminary, there in the Borders, graced by the now ruined abbeys of Melrose and Dryburgh, Jedburgh and Kelso. It was an area rich in pre-Reformation Church history.

Archbishop McDonald had twice tried to establish a national senior seminary. Around 1948 he had reached agreement with the bishops and put in an offer to buy the Grand Hotel in the Scores at St Andrews. He had discussed the scheme with Gordon Joseph.

The plan had been to combine with the Seminary Training College for male Catholic teachers – who, at that time, were admitted neither to Notre Dame nor to Craiglockhart College of Education. At the last moment (through an upsurge of anti-Catholic feeling which was fuelled by alleged commercial reasons from the retail shops) his offer was turned down, and the property was bought by the university as an additional students' hostel.

Undeterred, Archbishop McDonald then purchased a small farm on the outskirts of the town as a site for the senior seminary. At the last moment, Archbishop Campbell opted out, on the grounds that his name would be mud among his clergy if he did not build a diocesan seminary to replace the old St Peter's College at Bearsden which had been destroyed by fire some years before. This was an event which Gordon Joseph was convinced his predecessor firmly believed to have been a providential act of God!

So the high hopes for a national senior seminary were dashed. Nevertheless, Archbishop McDonald still wanted a seminary so that, in his own words, he would not have 'to go cap in hand to other seminaries to find places for his students'.

In 1952 the situation was critical. Indeed in that year there was one student for whom Gordon Joseph was unable to find a place.

Then, in the spring of 1953, the Archbishop saw an advertisement in *The Scotsman* newspaper for the sale of a mansion house, two miles from St Boswells and Melrose. He made enquiries through the diocesan lawyer, Norman Grant, and found that the property was indeed the mansion he had so long coveted. It was Drygrange.

It had been built in the late nineteenth century as a private house and had later been converted into a hotel. At the end of the Second World War it was purchased through the Churchill Trust for use as a rest home for retired hospital matrons and nurses.

Gordon Joseph sent the Catholic architect, Charles Gray, and Father Walter Glancy to visit the property incognito and report back. Most of the larger bedrooms had been partitioned and converted into two rooms each, leaving the large dining-room and lounges untouched. It might provide accommodation for a staff of half a dozen priests, four or five Sisters of Mercy to undertake the domestic work, and for perhaps 25 students. In all, the grounds extended to about 30 acres.

The asking price was only around £18,000, with an extra £3,000 for the extensive walled kitchen-garden and a long range of glass houses. However, the Archdiocese of St Andrews and Edinburgh was hard up financially. After studying the report, Gordon Joseph decided to take the plunge, nonetheless, and buy the property.

He wrote a pastoral letter (the only begging letter he could ever remember writing) explaining what he had done and why, and asking for donations to defray the cost. The laity, the priests and the religious rose to the occasion. Within a month there was enough to pay for the property. Big gifts and small, he acknowledged them all by hand, except for the anonymous donors for whom he could only express his gratitude in the daily Masses he regularly offered for those generous benefactors.

There was a great deal of anonymous generosity. One day the Archbishop came to the Cathedral. There he was met by the administrator, Monsignor Breen, who casually handed him a brown paper grocery bag, saying, 'I don't know what's in it. Someone handed it in and said: "Give it to the Archbishop for the seminary".'

When Gordon Joseph got back to St Bennet's, he opened it. It was stuffed with bank notes — 20, 30 years old, crumpled and from various banks. In all it amounted to £700 – someone's life savings!

Gordon Joseph got the keys for Drygrange and went down with Father Walter Glancy. They camped overnight inside the building with sandwiches and a flask of soup.

'And in the morning,' he remembered, 'on a little table in the lounge, I offered Mass with my eyes feasting over the beautiful River Leader and the gentle plains and rolling hills where 400 years ago, my brothers and sisters, religious and lay, had worked and prayed and joined in Mary's canticle of praise and thanksgiving that throbbed and echoed through my poor, muddled, yet ecstatically joyful mind:

> *My soul glorifies the Lord*
> *And my spirit rejoices in God my Saviour …*

'I felt the unity that bound me to Scotland's glorious past,' recalled Gordon Gray later, 'for my lips, though silent, were one in every *Magnificat* that, like the angelic choir on the first Christmas night, has risen through the uncharted expanses of God's universe to His home in heaven.'

St Andrew's College, Drygrange began its life on Our Lady's birthday, 8th September 1953. Gordon Joseph was there – as well as twelve students, four priests and four or five Sisters of Mercy. The chapel was the main lounge. The staff of priests, under the Rector, Father Roger Gallagher (a friend of Gordon Joseph's), were all fully qualified with excellent university degrees to prove their competence – from Rome, St Andrews, and, with the arrival of Father Karl Kruger in 1955, from the Institut Catholique in Paris.

Drygrange grew in numbers. Aberdeen, Argyll and the Isles, Motherwell (in the early 1970s) and Dunkeld sent students, until there were over 40 on the roll. There were also two students from France and one from Uganda.

Extensions became necessary – a convent for the Sisters, a new refectory, a chapel for the community, a library, a hall, several extra rooms, and an attic area designed to provide another ten rooms.

Drygrange trained over 100 priests in its life of 30 years – 30 difficult years during which Father John Barry (who later succeeded Father Gallagher as Rector) and the staff, including the spiritual director, the late Father Jock Dalrymple, had to steer a delicate course in the formation of future priests at a time when celibacy was being attacked and authority questioned.

CHAPTER 6

Second Vatican Council
(Session One)

THE year 1955 was marked by an important development. Along with Father Agnellus Andrew, Archbishop Gordon Gray, a trustee and board member, founded the Catholic Radio and Television Centre at Hatch End, Middlesex.

'I saw a lot of Agnellus, especially at Hatch End,' Cardinal Gray recalled later. 'My home in Edinburgh became his head-quarters where, in the evening, after a good meal, we relaxed and he would talk. He was never too busy to discuss, to advise and to leave me lifted in heart.'

Around the same time, a young judge and former Member of Parliament for East Edinburgh, moved with his family into White-house Terrace, not far from St Bennet's. John Wheatley (later Lord Justice Clerk) had been a firm friend from the time of Arch-bishop Gray's consecration in 1951. As a trustee of the Radio and Television Centre himself, he and the Archbishop often travelled together by train to meetings at Hatch End.

The story now moves forward to an evening in January 1959, when Archbishop Gordon Joseph Gray was driving to Nunraw Abbey in East Lothian for an ordination the following day. On the way, he switched on the car radio for the evening news bulletin.

The first item he heard was an announcement that Pope John XXIII had unexpectedly proclaimed that he had decided to call a General Council of the Church, to open in 1962.

The Archbishop was thrilled (perhaps, as he confessed later, for ulterior motives) – the trip wouldn't last long, but what a glorious opportunity to have a month or so in Rome, miles away from the routine work of the diocese. It would certainly be an exciting absence in Rome with an untroubled conscience.

Little did Gordon Joseph know what he was letting himself in for.

But there were other concerns at that time. Pope Pius XII, in his encyclical *Fidei Donum* of 1957, had appealed to bishops to send priests to the mission lands:

'A diocese should not be deaf to the appeal of the distant missions. The generosity of one poor diocese for another, even poorer, would not impoverish. God will not let himself be outdone in generosity.'

Pius XII was alerting his bishops to the wave of nationalism sweeping over Africa. Time was running out for the white colonial. If the Church was to survive, it was essential that young African men were trained to take over from white priests and bishops.

Gordon Gray was one of those who answered that appeal. Beginning in 1957, he was the first bishop in the world to send priests in response to *Fidei Donum*, first to Uganda and Nto Edino (part of the diocese of Calabar in eastern Nigeria) and later to Bauchi in the north of Nigeria. It is believed that Father Danny Simpson was the first *Fidei Donum* priest, and he was followed by around twelve others over the years, at a time when priests were in short supply in Scotland.

Although most of those first priests were sent to work with the Kiltegan Fathers at Calabar, one also went to Uganda with the White Fathers. As well as bringing Christianity to vast tracts of Nigeria, the experience of mission work changed all those priests and sisters who went to Bauchi, providing them with spiritual resources which they were able to employ for the benefit of Scottish Catholics on their return to this country.

'Never will I forget my first night in Calabar,' wrote the Cardinal of his first visit in February 1962, 'when I stayed with Father Danny Simpson. I awoke about six in the morning to the sound of quiet, prayerful voices outside my window. The words I could not understand, yet they had a familiar sound.

'Later, at breakfast, I asked Father Danny what had been happening. And his reply? "Oh, that was the catechist with the catechumens saying their morning prayers."

'"But," I asked, "it sounded at the end like a little litany." "Those," he said, "were the prayers for the conversion of Scotland, invocations to our Scottish saints."'

In Lagos, Gordon Joseph met the local Apostolic Delegate, Archbishop Sérgio Pignedoli, who encouraged him to send priests to Bauchi in northern Nigeria. Archbishop Pignedoli was an auxiliary bishop to the future Pope Paul VI when he was still Cardinal Montini of Milan.

Meanwhile the weeks and months that preceded the opening of the Second Vatican Council passed by. Archbishop Campbell, as president of the Scottish Episcopal Conference, was also a member of the preparatory commission.

He neither asked for his fellow bishops' thoughts, nor reported on what was under discussion at the meetings in Rome. Individually the bishops received a communication from the Vatican asking for suggestions for the agenda. To the best of his knowledge, only Gordon Joseph himself and Bishop Walsh of Aberdeen replied.

Two or three of Gordon Joseph's suggestions were recorded in the first volume of the transactions of Vatican II. Two or three others were omitted, including one on the revision of the Roman Breviary. Doubtless, many others had made the same suggestions, since the new Prayer of the Church was completely in accordance with what he had wished.

One of the other suggestions was a recommendation that priests who had left the priesthood, attempted marriage and incurred the responsibility of caring for a wife and family, should be dispensed from their priestly obligations and celibacy after, perhaps, ten years had elapsed.

A second suggestion was that, as was the practice with religious in parishes, a parish priest should be appointed for a specified period of perhaps six years and then return to the status of a curate.

Cardinal William Heard was a Presbyterian solicitor who had become a Roman Catholic and was a judge at the *Sacred Rota* (for marriage nullity cases) in Rome. When he learned of the second proposal from the Archbishop, he laughed at the very idea and emphasised that it could not possibly work in Italy where, when a parish priest was appointed, he frequently gave accommodation in the presbytery to his mother, sisters, his cousins and his aunts.

So the Scottish Bishops prepared, innocents at home, to become, when the Council opened, very much innocents abroad!

Little wonder. The Conference of Scottish Bishops was small and none of them was a top-class theologian. They were very much pastoral bishops doing a good job in their own little corner of the Vineyard.

Two or three days before the Council opened Gordon Joseph left for Rome. Bishop Stephen McGill (Argyll and the Isles) and Gordon Joseph opted to fly out on their own, since they did not like the idea of the whole Episcopal Conference flying out on the same plane, on which were travelling the Irish and most of the English and Scottish Bishops.

The two had also requested accommodation from the Holy See in one of the many hotels or pensions taken over primarily for Mission and Third World bishops. Their reasons were simply that they were attending an international council and did not want to spend their months in a little Scottish episcopal ghetto.

In many ways, theirs was a wise decision. The other bishops had agreed to stay at the Columbus Hotel. After a fortnight, they realised that, despite the convenience of proximity to the Vatican, they could not afford the cost of board and lodgings. They moved to a pension run by Sisters, had to arrange their own transport and, as Bishop Scanlan ruefully remarked, 'had horse-flesh for lunch and dinner on meat days!'

Bishop McGill and Archbishop Gordon Gray in contrast lived in comfort in the Globe Palace Hotel which was occupied almost entirely by bishops from Latin America, including quite a number from Argentina. All nice, friendly men, despite the difficulty of linguistic communication.

There was also Archbishop William Porter, Bishop Holland (a retired African missionary), Bishop Barbisotti, Vicar Apostolic of Esmeraldas in Equador, and an Italian Verona Father, a saintly man whose Latin was excellent and whose English was perfect. The two Scots always shared the same table and Bishop Barbisotti would go over the business discussed at the Council which they, less gifted in spoken Latin, had not fully followed.

When the Archbishop and Bishop McGill arrived in Rome, their hotel was hardly finished. But the owner spoke fluent

English – his wife had been educated at a convent school in England. The two Scots received VIP treatment, especially at meals. Granted it was noisy, being not far from the railway terminus and in the midst of an area where there were many hospitals.

Gordon Joseph and the other Scottish Bishops soon realised that they were pastoral bishops, not theologians, in the first full week of the Council, when they received a form to be filled in with names of the members of their Conference who were qualified to be members of various preparatory committees to draft documentation. They filled in the names – with the unspoken knowledge that it was for them rather a joke. But, after all, their invitation did give them their national identity. It was headed 'Caledonia'! That was something.

At night the sirens would shriek as ambulances and police cars raced past. The furniture was new and squeaked when the occupant moved in bed. But the rooms were more than adequate. Each of them had a pleasant bed-sitting room, a private and fully-fitted bathroom, and a little entrance hall to serve as a cloakroom. There were buses at the door if transport were needed – for the Council meetings the Vatican had laid on private buses which took them to St Peter's and brought them home for lunch. They occasionally invited their suffering Scottish episcopal colleagues for a meal – and how they envied the two.

After three weeks, during which the Archbishop and Bishop McGill said their Masses at the Church of San Lorenzo, the Vatican set up dozens of altars in one of the lounges of the hotel and there, each morning, they celebrated Mass (in those days *concelebration*, by which a number of priests could celebrate the same Mass together, had not been introduced).

They regularly rose early and booked an altar, each serving the other for Holy Mass. Then breakfast and out to the buses at about quarter to eight. They needed the early departure, for Roman traffic snarls were a familiar feature.

Normally they arrived at St Peter's around half eight, which gave time for a visit to the Blessed Sacrament or Confession if they wished. Then they prepared for the daily Mass at nine, which preceded the opening of Council business.

On one day each week they would have a Mass according to an ancient liturgy – the Eastern rite, the Abyssinian, Ukrainian and many others.

The Second Vatican Council opened on 11th October 1962. What Archbishop Gordon Joseph recalled most vividly was a very early rise, a hurried cup of coffee and, around six, into the bus for St Peter's.

He eventually found himself up many stairs in part of the Vatican museum with broken stone pillars and carved arches all around. He was there by seven to vest for the opening procession to be in place in the *aula* (hall) at nine for the Solemn Papal Mass.

It was a cope-and-mitre occasion. And it was a long, long wait. They moved off in procession almost an hour late, and when they entered the *aula* there was no question of finding one's own allotted seat. One sat where one could and politely refused to budge. Altogether, it was a greater spectacle than a spiritual experience and he was not alone in breathing a deep sigh of relief when the solemn *Ite missa est* (Go, the Mass is ended) was proclaimed.

In the evening, a great torchlight procession was scheduled. With a slight twinge of guilt, Gordon Joseph sat in the company of Bishop McGill, the Glasgow-born Franciscan broadcaster Father Agnellus Andrew, and Patrick O'Donovan of *The Observer*, watching the spectacle from their table at the Tre Scalini restaurant, sipping a glass of Chianti after a delicious Italian meal.

On the Friday morning everyone returned to St Peter's for the first working session. The opening Mass, notices from Archbishop Felici and, facing the assembly, a line of cardinals and bishops chosen from the *Curia* (the Vatican civil service) to head the ten Commissions that would regulate and finalise the constitutions and decrees.

Each bishop had before him a list of these names. Almost immediately (and unexpectedly) Cardinal Lienart asked to speak.

'We do not know the men proposed as candidates for membership of the commissions,' he said. 'The Episcopal Conferences must be given time to consider their suitability and make their own suggestions. Obviously, there will be no rubber-stamping!'

His intervention was seconded by Cardinal Frings and others.

Father Gordon Gray
~ Ordination Day, 15th June 1935 ~

Father Gordon Gray
~ at Blairs College, 1948 ~

(Argos Photographers, Edinburgh)

Father Gordon Gray
~ 1944 ~

Archbishop Gray
~ 1954 ~

Archbishop Gray blessing a child in Bauchi, North Nigeria
~ February 1962 ~

Dr Harry Whitley, Cardinal Gray and Episcopal Bishop Kenneth Carey
~ at St Giles Cathedral ~

*Cardinal Gray, outside St Peter's, Rome, when he was elevated to the Cardinalate,
with Pipe-Major Ronald Lawrie of the Glasgow City Police Pipe Band
~ 29th April 1969 ~*

*Cardinal Gray receives a relic of Saint Andrew from Pope Paul VI in Rome
~ May 1969 ~*

Cardinal Gray in the chapel at St Bennet's
~ May 1969 ~

A miraculous catch of six whiting
~ Outer Hebrides, 1970s ~

Cardinal Gray with Rusty
~ 8th August 1980 ~

*Cardinal Gray meets with the Very Revd Dr William Johnston to discuss the meeting
between Pope John Paul II and the Moderator
~ March 1982 ~*

*Pope John Paul II being welcomed by Cardinal Gray and Archbishop Winning
~ June 1982 ~*

(Stewart Ferguson)

'I am sure I have met many saints in my life. I think particularly of Pope Pius XII,
Pope Paul VI and Mother Teresa of Calcutta ... '
~ St Bennet's, Autumn 1982 ~

(Stewart Ferguson)

Cardinal Gray and the Dalai Lama
~ 1985 ~

Cardinal Gray with the Right Revd Professor Robert Craig
~ August 1986 ~

Cardinal Gray with Tom Farmer, CBE
~ St Mary's Cathedral, Edinburgh, 6th June 1993 ~

After some private consultations, it was announced that the ballot for the candidates for the commissions would be suspended until the following Tuesday.

Voting forms with the names of candidates were distributed, a request made that they be completed and handed in that same evening and the meeting adjourned.

The voting procedures were enormously complicated. Mathematically, there was the possibility of the names involving 400,000 votes. Consequently, everyone met on the Wednesday and the meetings were postponed until the following Saturday. So, one week was lost, but the principle was established that the Fathers of the Council would not be dictated to by the Curia.

Before the real work began with the opening of the debate on the *Schema on the Liturgy* on 22nd October, a message from the Council Fathers to the world (*A Statement to all Humanity*) was prepared, discussed, passed by a great majority and published. It was essentially a caring document from a Serving Church.

It was a psychological triumph on the part of the Central Commission that the Liturgy was chosen as the first subject for discussion. It touched the very heart of the Church's life and practice. It was a subject about which every bishop had some knowledge, about which each had an active interest.

It was not theologically demanding for the vast majority of pastoral bishops. It was like the first round in a boxing bout – an opportunity to size up the contestants and get the feel of the atmosphere.

To Archbishop Gordon Joseph, the great obstacle to free discussions during the Council – the insistence on the delivery of every intervention in Latin – was less apparent here than in the later debates. Everyone understood at least liturgical language and references and, even though less than fluent in the use of Latin in ordinary communication, they were more able to follow the discussions.

The Archbishop of St Andrews and Edinburgh did not speak during the Liturgical debate. He had two reasons for silence. The first, that one should not repeat what had been aired in a previous intervention. The second, that his Latin was poor and he had no one to put his English script into Latin.

For him, the Liturgical debates were fascinating, although often boring in their repetition and in frequently superficial but wordy interventions.

Although the Archbishop had asked Father John Barry, rector of Drygrange and a professor of Moral Theology and Canon Law, to accompany him to Rome, he found nothing to do and returned home after the first ten days. As soon as the sessions started, he had been excluded – only the bishops and the *periti* (formally appointed experts) were admitted. Father Barry could have been appointed a peritus, but that would have meant being away from Drygrange indefinitely.

The Scots had no *peritus* with them and no *latinist* (although they could have brought out one of the latter from Scotland quite easily). The Scots College staff could be of little help, since the Scottish Bishops were staying in hotels in the city and the College staff, for half the duration of the Council, were in residence at the College villa in the cool of the Alban Hills at Merino, about 20 miles out of the heat of Rome.

So even if the Scots had wished to make an intervention from the Council floor, they had no help to ensure that the text was in reasonable Latin form.

Those who could speak fluently in Latin were, for the most part, members of the Curia, or former university or seminary professors. The Scots pastoral bishops, who could have contributed so much of real importance to a Pastoral Council, were all too frequently silenced through the rule of speaking in Latin.

'I recall two instances,' Cardinal Gray remembered – 'Cardinal Cushing of Boston spoke once, in impeccable Latin, obviously written for him by an American peritus. It is said that, on his return to Boston, he was met by an army of journalists who asked "Cardinal, you spoke at the Council; what did you say?" According to some reports, he replied, "I don't know. You see, I was speaking in Latin!"'

The second instance is purely personal. Archbishop Gray prepared three interventions. He thought they were all quite sensible, pastoral and intended to underline the problems that the Council theme under discussion would give rise to in a Protestant country such as Scotland. The first concerned the holiness of the laity and the other two referred to Ecumenism.

'On the first occasion my name was called at the beginning of the Assembly to speak. I went over my text. Each time I read it, I was more ashamed of my classroom Latin. I got cold feet and told Cardinal John Krol, who was a member of the Secretariat, that I would hand in my script, but would not speak. He was annoyed and twice came back to me in the *aula* (hall) to insist that I should. I still refused. Lately, I read my three prepared interventions in the *acta* (proceedings) of Vatican II and regret that I did not voice them publicly.

'The rule of Latin only,' added Cardinal Gray, 'resulted in a succession of set speeches and the absence of real dialogue. The only chance of disagreement available was through submitting *modi* (requests for modification in the wording of a text).

'At Vatican II, many voices were muted that might have uttered valuable and positive pastoral thoughts. Had they been uttered, the aftermath of Vatican II might have been less traumatic.'

Gordon Joseph enjoyed the 328 speeches on the Liturgy that filled the days from 22nd October until 13th November – at least, the vast majority. Sometimes, in the airless atmosphere of the *aula*, he and the other bishops struggled against sleep! And, around eleven o' clock, it was a relief to slip away quietly to the two bars set up in the sacristies, nicknamed the *Bar-Jonah* and the *Bar-Abbas* for a reviving cup of coffee and a chat.

It made Gordon Joseph aware as never before – a fact he remembered for the rest of his life – that more useful discussion can take place informally at a coffee-break than in a structured and organised meeting.

The debate on the Liturgy continued to 14th November, when, by a massive majority, the Council Fathers approved a general plan for the updating of the Liturgy – to be finalised at the Second Session. Only 46 out of 2,215 voted *non placet*.

It has to be remembered that the constitutions, decrees and declarations of Vatican II that were eventually approved were no more than blueprints. In every case, post-conciliar congregations and commissions were entrusted with the work of putting flesh on the bones.

Gordon Joseph had intimate knowledge of the Liturgical Constitution. The Constitution was accepted in its present form (*De Sacra Liturgia*) by 2,158 votes to 19. But it only set out principles for reform.

'I do not think that the Fathers present at Vatican II,' said Cardinal Gray in later years, 'would have approved of all the changes that have taken place through the work of the Consilium and the Congregation for Divine Worship. They have gone far further than was ever expected – or, I believe, intended.'

Gordon Joseph would later regret that the Tridentine Mass was not allowed to die a natural death, instead of being summarily executed; but he firmly believed that the simplification of the ceremonial, the participation of the laity, the virtual death of Latin now replaced by the vernacular, was a step forward in the prayer life of the Church and more suited to the mentality and outlook of the younger generation.

He did, however, point to a number of losses in the process of liturgical change – the sacral atmosphere of the Liturgy, the traditional, emotional feeling that a solemn liturgy was indeed Divine Worship.

Having temporarily disposed of the Liturgy, the Fathers of the Council turned their thoughts to Revelation.

'I was out of my depth,' confessed the Cardinal. 'At college in 1929-35, Scripture was cautiously taught and covered little more than cautious *exegesis* (exposition). Moreover, I missed two years of our superficial lectures since I was studying for a London University degree in my spare time.

'All I remember was that the debate was a hot one! Cardinal Alfredo Ottaviani, supported by very traditional scriptural scholars, spoke vehemently and forcibly in favour of the schema produced by himself and his Theological Commission.

'The Jesuit fathers from the Biblical Institute – Cardinal Bea, Cardinal Ruffini, Karl Rahner and Father Ratzinger – as vehemently campaigned against it and were backed up by a strong force of the younger and pastoral bishops, whose scriptural studies had been influenced by the Encyclical of Pope Pius XII, *Divino Afflanti Spiritu.*'

With many others, Archbishop Gordon Joseph Gray wondered whose voice was the more important in the Church – that of the bishops, the teaching Church, or the theologians. This was a dilemma that arose on too many occasions when the theologians talked too loudly and as if with an infallible voice.

On 20th November, Archbishop Felici was authorised to put a motion to the vote: 'Would the Fathers continue discussion on the present schema?'

The *placet* and *non placet* vote was worded so ambiguously that many were uncertain which way their vote would weigh the outcome – for or against. However, Council rules about a two-thirds majority (which Gordon Joseph never really understood) prevailed, and it was decided that the debate should continue, chapter by chapter.

Analysed, it meant that only 38 per cent of the voters were in favour of continuing with the schema, but those opposed to it had not gained the necessary two-thirds majority.

'I recalled the voting procedure,' said the Cardinal later, 'when we in Scotland had a referendum on the setting up of a Scottish Assembly. Those in favour failed, by a comparatively small margin of the votes cast, to get a two-thirds majority and the cause was lost – for the time being.'

However, Pope John XXIII had seen the amber light turning to red. It was announced that he had decided to set up a special mixed Commission to re-write the whole schema and postpone further debate.

The next theme of debate was 'The Communication Media'. This brought great satisfaction to Gordon Joseph. For years he had been a member of the Central Religious Advisory Committee for the BBC and, as a friend of Bishop Agnellus Andrew, had been his principal adviser on the setting-up of the Radio and Television Centre at Hatch End in 1955. For his part, Agnellus Andrew had been Gordon Joseph's coach in radio speaking techniques.

It was later said that the *Decree on Communications* was one of the weakest documents of Vatican II, but the schema was by no means the same as the decree. The Decree, in Gordon Joseph's opinion, was far from weak. It was 'a long overdue acknowledgement from Rome,' wrote the Archbishop, 'of the importance of the media, and a blueprint that helped us greatly in the compilation of the *Pastoral Instruction on Communications* which was issued in 1971 (*Communio et Progressio*) in which I was intimately and deeply involved.' Indeed, for two years he chaired the relevant Commission.

On the other hand, the Archbishop was the first to admit that 'Vatican Press communications have always been appalling, and that (despite dozens of new telephones and typewriters) the Council Press Office had no idea of the requirements or of the importance of the world press and communication media that flocked to Rome. It treated the media like children. It resented its presence and, when it eventually issued press reports, they were inadequate, superficial and out of date. The journalists had their contacts and, it would seem, bishops held their own private press conferences!'

The next schema to be discussed was on *Unity with the Orthodox Churches*. The discussion did not last long and it was quickly voted out, to be re-written in a wider context by a joint Commission for the Eastern Churches.

There was less and less time left before the Council adjourned on 8th December. The Presidency decided that the Council would now (1st December) proceed to the schema *De Ecclesia* (The Church) which Gordon Joseph thought to be a rather stupid proposal. *De Ecclesia* was the very hub of a wheel whose spokes were the decrees and declarations, and whose rim would eventually be *The Church in the Modern World.* Many thought likewise. So did Cardinal Ottaviani, who controlled the Holy Office.

Attached to the schema *De Ecclesia* was a long chapter on Our Blessed Lady, which some had hoped might be issued as a separate document. Others were opposed to its being given too much prominence – for ecumenical reasons.

Cardinal Ottaviani proposed, however, that the chapter on Our Lady should occupy the last few remaining days of the first Session.

'Poor Ottaviani,' recalled Gordon Joseph, 'was a die-hard curialist of the old brigade, a faithful son of the Church who, I am sure, deeply resented this ecclesiastically democratic assembly of Council Fathers, and held aloft a banner marked "No change!" Had someone else proposed his motion, it might well have been accepted.'

So, the debate on the schema *De Ecclesia* began on 1st December, as the last days of Session One passed by. Return flights from Rome were joyfully booked.

It had been a long, hard voyage through sometimes rough, uncharted waters, with a crew unaccustomed to manning a ship at sea.

Gordon Joseph returned home on 8th December, relieved to be back to his old pastoral role, but a little wiser and humbler than when he had arrived in Rome ten weeks before.

CHAPTER 7

Vatican II – The Interim
(between Session One and Two)

ARCHBISHOP Gordon Joseph had left for the Council with the press and photographers at Turnhouse airport. In marked contrast, he returned very quietly. It was a Thursday. He had telephoned from Heathrow to arrange for the car to pick him up at Turnhouse.

No reply from St Bennet's. Then he remembered – the Sisters would be at St Margaret's Convent for confessions and no one would be in the house. So, after collecting his luggage at the airport, he took a taxi. Suddenly he realised he had no British money for the fare!

The taxi arrived at St Bennet's – no reply – so he asked the driver to take him to his mother's house at 3, St Catherine Place, borrowed some money to pay the fare, and relaxed. Then, later, he phoned St Bennet's and Sister Carmella came along with the car and drove him home.

It was not destined to be an easy year. Quite apart from the routine work (which was heavy), the situation in Aberdeen was heading for a crisis.

Bishop Francis Walsh, a friend of his, had a heart of gold. A good lady called Mrs McKenzie, wife of a Church of Scotland minister, wanted to become a Catholic. According to her, life had become intolerable and she was shown the door. She came to Bishop Walsh, who would never see anyone homeless. He took her in, instructed her and, finally, received her into the Catholic Church.

Mrs McKenzie stayed on in the presbytery and the bishop's housekeeper then left. The new convert was highly-strung. She could not be left alone, with the result that the Bishop, in the kindness of his heart, took her with him in the car when visiting the parishes in his widespread diocese.

Her intrusion was resented and gradually became a source of scandal. Complaints were sent to the Apostolic Delegate, Archbishop O'Hara, an American (and himself, very excitable and precipitate).

As Metropolitan Archbishop, Gordon Joseph found himself involved, but, despite his endeavours to be a peace-maker, the situation exploded. The two, Bishop Walsh and the Delegate, met at St Bennet's over a good meal. He left them alone.

On his return he found Archbishop O'Hara raging. He demanded that Gordon Joseph should get on the phone to Rome so that he could send a coded message to the effect that the bishop should be immediately retired.

In the middle of the row, Bishop Walsh walked out. Gordon Joseph decided to play for time and, by two in the morning, had convinced the Delegate that he couldn't get through to the Secretariat of State. At around seven Gordon Joseph phoned St Mary's Cathedral, Edinburgh in the hope that the Bishop might have stayed there for the night. He had, but had caught a very early train back to Aberdeen.

Eventually, Gordon Joseph got the Delegate back to London, went up to Aberdeen, but got nowhere with the Bishop. Then he went down to London, with a similar result. On 22nd July Bishop Walsh resigned. For a time he lived in Dublin and then moved to England, to Grantham near Cambridge, where he lived in a caravan set up in a farmyard. He died there on 27th October 1974.

'I went down to his Requiem Mass and buried him,' recalled Cardinal Gray. 'He was a great man, full of zeal and with a big heart, but sorely lacking in prudence and discretion. My sorrow was that, despite my best efforts to effect an understanding and reconciliation between himself, Rome and the Delegate, I failed.

'Because I pleaded with him to give obedience to Rome and promised to make financial provision for the maintenance of Mrs McKenzie, he completely misinterpreted my intentions, went his own way and never again communicated with me.'

To increase Gordon Joseph's despondency, when Bishop Walsh's resignation had been accepted by the Pope on 12th September 1963, and his *translation* (transfer) to the Titular See of Birta was announced, the Archbishop of St Andrews and Edinburgh was appointed apostolic administrator for the diocese of Aberdeen, a position he held until 8th December 1964, when Father Michael Foylan was nominated bishop.

An apostolic administrator, at least before the new Code of Canon Law was published, had full responsibilities for the running of the diocese, but could not appoint a vicar-general to deal with the day-to-day business.

Consequently, during two sessions of the Vatican Council, Gordon Joseph had to fly back to Edinburgh each fortnight on a Friday morning, spend the Saturday dealing with dispensations and other urgent matters in Aberdeen, and return to Rome for the Sunday evening. Little wonder that in 1964 he developed a duodenal ulcer!

Perhaps 1963 was his worst year, for on 22nd July, the very day on which Bishop Walsh resigned, Archbishop Campbell of Glasgow died on pilgrimage in Lourdes. He was succeeded on 29th January 1964 by Bishop Scanlan of Motherwell, an old and dear friend of Gordon Joseph's, who by then had been elected President of the Scottish Episcopal Conference.

The Archbishop was faced by one other worrying situation – a strange and incredible problem. The priest concerned came to see the Archbishop at St Bennet's. He took out a metal crucifix about eight inches high.

'When I am praying,' he told Gordon Joseph, 'I have seen the Sacred Host come from nowhere and rest in this crucifix. I have seen blood flowing from the wounds on the hands of Our Lord in this crucifix. I have seen the *stigmata* (the wounds of Christ).'

'I believe he was speaking the truth,' wrote the Cardinal later. 'Who am I to say – is it possible? Could it happen? Sincerely, he believed what he said. God works in mysterious ways. I myself will remain curious, until I enter eternity, to know what it was all about, how it happened and why? I am just a little sceptical when I read of people, apparently holy, who have received the stigmata and seen visions! A bishop's life? Most people would not believe the facts!'

*   *   *

The world was much saddened by the death of Pope John XXIII on 23rd June 1963. To Gordon Joseph, Pope John had always been rather an enigma. He popularised the Papacy, especially among non-Catholics. He was very human in his appearance – short, stocky and stout, joking and smiling. He was so different in manner and dignity from his wonderful, learned, ascetic and much misunderstood predecessor, Pius XII.

Pope John was outwardly so democratic, yet at least twice he over-ruled the Council. He gave the impression of homeliness, simplicity and of being one who avoided pomp or ceremony.

'Yet – read his diary,' pointed out Cardinal Gray in later years, 'his requests to his sisters to send him some more red socks when he was Nuncio in Paris and a Cardinal! And, at the great ceremonies in Rome, he was the last of the Popes I knew, to enter the Basilica of St Peter's, smiling at and blessing the crowds from the *sedia gestatoria* (processional chair).'

In calling the Second Vatican Council, Pope John XXIII may have opened the window of the Vatican to let in fresh air, but he went to God without having to close them just a little.

It was to Paul VI that he left the legacy of implementing the Council he had begun.

'And how magnificently Paul VI fulfilled his duties,' added Cardinal Gray. 'He suffered, but quietly, gently and unacclaimed. He worked miracles that would have been beyond the power of his predecessor, John.'

Those who knew Gordon Gray well, always understood that Paul VI was his favourite Pope – he admired that patient suffering and was aware of the love which Paul VI had for him personally, and for the people of Scotland.

CHAPTER 8

*Vatican II
(Session Two)*

ON 27th September 1963, Gordon Joseph left Edinburgh for Rome and met up with Bishop McGill at Heathrow. They had been booked in by the Vatican at a different hotel – the Cesare Augusto near Ponte Milvio. The accommodation was good – much the same as in their previous hotel. The food, however, was indifferent and many a morning the two left without coffee or a roll because the milkman or the baker happened to be late. But they were – more or less – with their old friends, the Argentinians.

The buses took them each morning to St Peter's and they enjoyed their stay. They were only a mile from the new Scots College which was then under construction. There were shops near at hand and, with a walk, they could quickly get into the heart of Rome, since buses were frequent.

The new Session began on 29th September. There had been speculation as to whether or not the new Pope, Paul VI, would continue the Council or suspend it *sine die.*

He did not suspend it and, moreover, re-emphasised the aims of his predecessor in his opening address and, above all, the need for unity and reconciliation among Christian denominations.

His *mea culpa* (I am sorry) was clear and humble. The Roman Catholic Church was to blame for the Robe of Christ rent in two. It was a brilliant address that shocked some and pleased most. Some did not like the *mea culpa*. However, it emphasised the intention of Paul VI to pursue the work of the Council to the end, and – as time would prove – to implement its findings when those findings 'were not always what he, as a pastoral priest, might have wished', concluded the Cardinal in his later years.

He was the Pope who signed the declarations, decrees and

constitutions, and for him they were sacrosanct. Although Pope, he had been (and remained in his elevated position), still a Father of the Council.

Once there was a gleam of hope. Technicians came into the *aula* and experimented with short-wave radio transmission of the proceedings, which would have allowed for simultaneous translation. But, apparently, the technicians could not confine the broadcast within the walls of the Vatican and the idea was dropped.

'Although inadequate and unprepared to participate in such a great event,' pointed out Cardinal Gray twenty years later, 'my presence, so far as I was concerned, was not wasted. I received new insights into the teaching of the Church, into its ability to remain unchanged in doctrine, yet adapt itself to preach the Gospel intelligently in an ever-changing world. It changed me.

'I thank God for a new vision of the width and breadth and depth of the Divine work of Redemption. It gave a new dimension to the decision I had taken after the publication of *Fidei Donum* (Gift of Faith), to see the missionary Church as an essential element in my own episcopal responsibilities.'

Well did Gordon Joseph remember Wednesday 27th November 1963, when he offered the Council Mass at the little temporary altar at the Cardinals' end of the great rows of seating that rose high on either side of the *aula*, the whole length of the Basilica.

Himself, alone – except for the Papal master of ceremonies; the old Latin Tridentine Mass; his congregation a microcosm of the Church, more than two and a half thousand souls; bishops and cardinals from every corner of the world, together with hundreds of *periti* and observers.

'It was, for me,' Cardinal Gray stated later, 'one of the greatest and most moving occasions in my life as a priest. There I stood, the spokesman for the universal Church, standing in the place of Our Lord at the altar to renew the Sacrifice of Calvary. Some memories fade. That will never fade.'

CHAPTER 9

Implementing Vatican II

THE Council ended with great ceremonial, great hope, great relief for most, and the distribution of a ring to all the Fathers who had participated. Being a member of Vatican Congregations gave Gordon Joseph a greater insight into the intricacies of the administration of the Roman Catholic Church than did the Vatican Council itself.

The Pope himself, for example, cannot be personally involved in the day-to-day problems and discussions that arise in a world-wide Church. He must delegate. Even his correspondence must be opened, read and answered through the Secretariat of State.

Letters sent by the thousands of correspondents receive a reply, often in an accepted formula, including the blessing of the Holy Father. Some are referred for consideration to the bishop of the diocese from which they emanate. Many are forwarded to the congregations, commissions and councils to which are entrusted specific areas of the Church's concerns.

Before and during Vatican II, many bishops resented the power of the various Curial *dicasteries* (departments). They felt that they were little acquainted with the pastoral problems of diocesan bishops; that their members, trained for the diplomatic service of the Church, frequently acted without consultation with the bishops, who might be attacked by dissenters or accused because of their pastoral practice and decisions.

It was felt, by many, that the Curia (Vatican civil service) was too powerful, too independent and autonomous. They were entrusted to speak and to make decisions in the name of the Holy Father. Clearly, there could be no appeal to one who could not possibly study every episcopal grievance. There was and is a court of appeal (known as *The Supreme Segnatura*), but its membership is largely composed of Curial officials from other congregations.

Pope Paul VI recognised the problem and, following the mind of the Fathers of the Council, decided to appoint pastoral bishops from various parts of the world to membership of the various dicasteries. It was a good reform and, whilst the blueprints of Vatican II were being studied, expounded and prepared for implementation, it proved of great value.

'However, the Prefects in positions of authority, can sometimes assume dictatorial attitudes,' Cardinal Gray pointed out later. 'Considerable damage can be done to the Church by the appointment of men to top Curial posts who do not acknowledge that they are not infallible, nor endowed with authority to over-rule the decisions of bishops ordained to rule, sanctify and teach in the diocese entrusted to their pastoral care.'

Like Gordon Joseph, after the Council had ended, most bishops made the round of deaneries and parishes to relate the events of Vatican II. They urged their priests, religious and laity to read and implement its documentation, to establish diocesan and national commissions to study and issue guidelines.

'There was expectation in the air and new organisations were launched to plan renewal programmes,' commented the Cardinal 'There were the progressives who read more into the constitutions, decrees and declarations than the less forward-looking Fathers, and some impatient clergy and laity who wanted everything done today and not tomorrow.

'Clearly the Liturgy, Ecumenism and the Role of the Laity were areas to which enthusiasts (who had read those parts of the documentation that appealed to them) demanded immediate attention. They did not appreciate that Vatican II had to be seen and studied, not as isolated documents, but as a whole.'

Gordon Joseph's favourite way of representing the Council was to refer to it as a wheel. The Constitution on the Church was the hub; the decrees and declarations were the spokes emerging from the hub, encircled and held together by the rim – *The Pastoral Constitution on the Church in the Modern World.* He tried to emphasise the interaction of the many parts, each part with its own special function, but all bound together in unity for the proper efficiency and working of the whole body.

Gradually, the Scottish Episcopal Conference established diocesan and national commissions on Liturgy, Education, Vocations, Christian Unity, Communications and, of course, a more structured organisation for the Lay Apostolate. No doubt they were all in accordance with the Roman organisations from which they were conceived and were born. But in Scotland, a small country with approximately 800,000 Catholics and only eight dioceses, Archbishop Gordon Joseph did not believe that the spiritual dividends derived would be sufficient to outweigh the crippling overdrafts the bishops would have to meet.

'I admit that I was cautious,' recalled the Cardinal, 'and I believe I was right. In many areas of the Church elsewhere, too much was done too soon. Because we in Scotland were slower than others, the withdrawal symptoms were less violent.'

Lent 1965 was a crucial period for Scottish Catholics. The Mass in English (the vernacular) was introduced with some trepidation. Mass facing the people was also introduced and this necessitated sometimes costly architectural reorganisation.

'I am confident,' said the Archbishop, 'that in a few months time, when the novelty of the changes has disappeared, our assistance at Mass will be a richer and deeper spiritual experience.'

In 1965 Gordon Joseph made his second visit to Nigeria. It was a useful visit, since by then the Scottish volunteer priests had moved from Calabar to Bauchi. He toured the province, under the guidance of Father Danny Simpson, and realised the potential of their undertaking.

The welcome he received in the village of Nto Edino was triumphal. There were cheers and gunfire, speeches and dances. Two days later he was presented with gifts – three sheep, several cocks, a pile of yams, a basin of eggs, two cases of beer, a four-gallon carafe of palm wine and a tin of cigarettes.

But there were moments of sadness, too, such as he described to the Union of Catholic Mothers rally in Glasgow early in 1968:

'I saw little children rummaging for food in the garbage heaps, fighting for decaying, putrid morsels, like their foraging companions, the vultures, did. And another time, little children,

eyes gleaming, grasping the crusts we'd left for the birds after a
picnic lunch at a bush mission; grasping them, hugging them,
gazing at them, hardly believing their treasure was real; afraid
to eat them because – then they'd be gone and gnawing hunger
would return.'

One day they visited Gambar, after pushing the car across
dried-up streams, and saw a couple of bungalows in a few acres
of bush land that had been occupied by British supervisors of a tin-
mine in the district (now exhausted) and which were up for sale.

The Archbishop agreed to purchase them: fortunately, because
to that district came the Ursulines of Jesus to found a hospital
and clinic. There, in place of a tumbledown mud-built chapel,
there is today an extensive compound with a training centre for
catechists, a hospital and centre for instructing local people in
their faith, in hygiene and in trades, and a rapidly-increasing
congregation of Christians. It was the greatest achievement of
the *Fidei Donum* priests and Sisters from the archdiocese of St
Andrews and Edinburgh. The development gave the Archbishop
great joy and the conviction that their little sacrifice in staffing and
resources had not been in vain, and the diocese's contribution in
adopting a territory to staff and finance it for over 20 years was
unique.

For Gordon Joseph came a particular pleasure when, on 30th
June 1967, he was honoured by his *alma mater*, the University of
St Andrews, with the degree of Doctor of Divinity. Joining him
was his former fellow-student, Professor Robert Craig, then acting
Principal of the University College of Rhodesia. Receiving the
degree of Doctor of Laws were Henry Moore, the sculptor, and
the Secretary of State for Scotland, William Ross.

And there were always moments when his conscience pricked
the Archbishop, such as the Saturday before Christmas 1967, as he
drove himself in comparative comfort through the city to his
Cathedral. In the streets he saw young men and women, university students, standing in the busy shopping centres.

'It was a cold day,' he recalled, 'the east winds were laced with
ice. In one hand they held a collecting box; in the other, a banner
– *War on Want.* Above the letters was the picture of a shrivelled
living child skeleton. How many passed by? I felt ashamed. I

should have been there on the cold icy crossroads begging for Christ. I passed by.'

Yet another milestone in his career came on 21st January 1968, when Gordon Joseph preached from the John Knox pulpit, the first Roman Catholic to do so since the Reformation. In his sermon he suggested that there were four levels in which work for Christian Unity could be pursued – within people themselves, 'focussing a searchlight on our souls'; mutual understanding born of study and dialogue; united common Christian action by the Christian community; finally, through prayer. He ended by emphasising that 'surely and slowly, four centuries of painful estrangement – often marked by bitterness and blood – are coming to an end'.

But there were other, internal problems facing the Catholic Church in the years after the Second Vatican Council:

'Devolution from central authority,' wrote Archbishop Gordon Gray, 'can lead to a multiplicity of new structures at local level. Wide consultation can lead to an avalanche of paper descending through the letter-box; the desire for dialogue can lead to a profusion of meetings and a subsequent loss of time. The crisis of authority has made itself felt in every sphere of life. Inevitably, since authority is basic to our whole system of belief.

'There is confusion between the acceptance of authority (with the corresponding obedience which it involves) and personal freedom – the obligation to follow the individual conscience.

'There is a greater delicacy in the exercise of authority that can be misinterpreted as a lack of confidence on the part of authority itself. And in an age of ceaseless questioning, many of the disciplinary laws of the Church are questioned, sometimes opposed. So, for example, the centuries-old rule of a celibate priesthood in the Western Church.

'Of course, a distorted picture emerges, for always the voices of the extremist protagonists are the loudest. The appearance so often given in the press and on television – of a Church combating widespread unrest, ceaseless controversy, confusion, revolt – is untrue. The vast majority of Roman Catholics have quietly and gratefully accepted the consequences of Vatican II's renewal.'

When Pope Paul VI finally issued his encyclical, *Humanae*

Vitae, on 25th July 1968 (to a world watching events in Czechoslovakia and Biafra deteriorate daily), every bishop in the world faced perhaps his most sensitive problem as the spiritual leader of his diocese. Not least Archbishop Gordon Gray and his fellow Scottish Bishops.

World public opinion had prepared itself for a change in the Vatican's attitude to birth regulation, encouraged by the leak of the recommendations of the Papal Commission on Birth Control. The view of 53 out of the original 57 lay and clerical members was that 'mechanical' methods of birth control – and even the pill, taken on a permanent basis (subject to medical advice) – were acceptable. In the event, the encyclical re-stated traditional doctrine and condemned 'artificial' methods of birth regulation.

In October 1968, the bishops of Scotland issued a pastoral letter, which confirmed to Catholics that the Pope's teaching in *Humanae Vitae* clearly condemned the use of artificial methods of birth control as evil and that his authority in this matter could not be over-ridden by the primacy of individual conscience. In Scotland, unlike south of the Border, there was scarcely a ripple of public protest.

Among the Scottish Catholic laity there was honest concern and much heart-searching in an effort to be loyal to Papal teaching and the guidance of the bishops. But often, the pressure of events and weariness at prolonged controversy, resulted in married couples having recourse to the prayerful judgement of their individual conscience as the final arbiter of right action under God. In these circumstances, techniques other than the 'rhythm method' were intrinsically evil, but might not necessarily be sinful.

In late 1968, no doubt as a result of his missionary effort in Nigeria, Archbishop Gordon Joseph was appointed a member of the Sacred Congregation for the Evangelisation of Peoples.

Membership of other Vatican bodies would follow – in 1976 he was an observer on the Pontifical Commission for Social Communication, since Archbishop Beck of Liverpool, the only member from Great Britain and Ireland, was ill. Not long after, he was appointed a member of the Commission, which numbered around 70 members and consultors from all parts of the world.

CHAPTER 10

Cardinal

IT was the morning of the 28th of March 1969, at half past ten. Archbishop Gray was at his desk in his study at St Bennet's. He had a busy day in front of him as usual, with letters needing replies and visitors expected.

The telephone rang, breaking the silence. It was the Apostolic Delegate, calling from London. Archbishop Eugenio Cardinale began by mentioning a fairly minor matter over which they had corresponded and had a bit of an argument about. Then he said: 'I didn't phone you up about that really. It's just that there's an announcement coming out at 12 o'clock and I thought I'd better read it over to you before you hear it on the radio.'

Gordon Joseph took him to be referring to some new edict. Then the Apostolic Delegate read something in Latin, and the name 'Gordon Joseph Gray' came into it.

'Here, your Excellency,' Gordon Joseph said, 'read that again – I didn't catch it properly.'

And he re-read it. It was a formal proclamation announcing that there was to be a new Cardinal – Gordon Joseph Gray. Then he broke into English, adding his congratulations.

'Good heavens,' said Gordon Joseph, 'I don't believe it.'

The Delegate just laughed and put down the phone.

Immediately Cardinal-elect Gordon Joseph Gray sent for his domestic staff. He broke the news to Sister Zita and Sister Carmella and then telephoned his 86-year old mother.

The first to congratulate him was his good friend Archbishop Scanlan of Glasgow, who had also been notified by the Apostolic Delegate. After that the telephone began to ring continuously and the telegrams began to arrive.

'It was such a shock that I have not recovered my wits yet,' Gordon Joseph admitted to the reporters who had come to St Bennet's on 28th March 1969 to hear his reactions at being made a Cardinal.

'The Holy Father,' he added, 'has shown a signal honour to Scotland and I am very proud that it has been bestowed on my country.'

The Church of Scotland, the Episcopal Church and the Scottish Council of Churches all welcomed the appointment, which was described in the press as 'the biggest thing that has happened in years to Scotland's Roman Catholics, and perhaps to all Scottish Christians.'

Dr Nevile Davidson, who had (it will be remembered) been one of the guests at the celebratory lunch when Gordon Gray was made an Archbishop, commented in *Life and Work*:

'A new spirit of tolerance is abroad .... This warmth of feeling, however, is due in no small part to the character and personality of the new Cardinal himself. Few can have done more than Archbishop Gordon Gray to promote happy and fraternal relationships with other Churches in Scotland.'

But there were also voices of dissent. The Revd Neil MacLeod, Convenor of the Public Questions, Religion and Morals Committee of the Free Church of Scotland said: 'The Church of Rome has never made any secret of the fact that one of her great ambitions is to bring Great Britain back into subjection to the papacy. She has always pursued her ambitions with great subtlety and this appointment must be viewed in that light.'

'It is a retrograde step to darkness instead of light,' commented the Revd Jack Glass of the Zion Baptist Church in Glasgow, 'to slavery instead of liberty and superstition instead of truth.'

The new Cardinal told the press: 'I welcome the change in attitude towards Christian unity achieved over the past ten or twenty years. I see something definite and tangible in it.'

Gordon Gray was the fifth Scottish Cardinal. After Walter Wardlaw in the fourteenth century (appointed by the anti-pope), the first Catholic Cardinal was David Beaton (1494-1546), followed by Henry Benedict Maria Clement Stuart (1725-1807), brother of Prince Charles Edward Stuart. A significant figure for Scotland was Charles Erskine, born in Rome in 1739. In 1803, while Scotland was still a mission country, he was made Cardinal Protector of Scotland. He died in Paris in 1811. William Theodore Heard (1884-1973), a canon lawyer, was based in Rome as Dean of the *Sacred Rota*, the supreme court of appeal for declarations of marriage nullity.

There was, of course, intense speculation at the time as to the reason for the new Cardinal's appointment. While some members of the press suggested it was Gordon Gray's leadership in firmly supporting the Pope's position on birth control as expressed in the encyclical *Humanae Vitae* (July 1968) and others asked if the Red Hat was not a sign of recognition for the growing Scottish Nationalist movement, it emerged that there were four considerations that had merited the honour – his initiative in sending priests to Nigeria; his encouragement for the ecumenical movement, and his international work for the Church, particularly for the International Commission on the English in the Liturgy. Lastly, it was a means for the Vatican to re-emphasise that the Scottish Church was a separate entity, not a subsidiary part of the Church in England and Wales.

One of the first of his duties as Cardinal was to preach two days later at the evening service at St Mary's Episcopal Cathedral in Edinburgh – an engagement arranged weeks before.

A handful of demonstrators from the Protestant Action Society had picketed the entrance to the Cathedral. They carried placards urging members of the congregation to 'Remember 1690' and proclaiming 'We want Martyrs, not Traitors'.

Just as the Cardinal began to preach, the first demonstrators, who had been sitting in the congregation, marched out. As he was speaking of his gratitude at his warm welcome to St Mary's, a young woman dressed in a scarlet coat, marched up the aisle mumbling, and shouted from the door of the church, 'We don't want unity. We will fight to keep Scotland Protestant'. During a later part of his sermon, another woman walked out down the aisle shouting 'To Hell with the Pope.'

In reply, the Cardinal continued, 'If we are worthy to be called Christians, we must be prepared, not only to contemplate the sufferings of Christ, but to suffer with Christ. We must be prepared, not only to contemplate the love of Christ, but to love Christ.' He added that the way towards Church Unity was to allow the unimportant differences between Churches to be absorbed and forgotten in the passionate love of Christ.

Greeted then by a number of hecklers, he later said: 'That sort of minor demonstration won't harm the movement towards Church unity.'

Although a liberal in ecumenical affairs, Cardinal Gray characterised himself as a conservative on issues such as birth-control and married priests:

'I have no doubt that the Pope's decision on birth-control was not only the right decision, but the *only* decision he could have made.

'There are two types of law in relation to the Church, and they are divine and natural laws which cannot be changed. Then there are secular laws which are more the Church's own rules.

'Birth-control is a subject concerned with the first category. It relates to the sanctity of human life – even in its most initial form – and therefore is unchangeable.

'The question of married priests is a matter for the second category. It is a Church law and therefore subject to change if the Church sees fit.

'I don't believe that marriage within the priesthood is desirable, in the sense that the same dedication and self-sacrifice can be given to the job in hand. But the point is, there might well come a time when it might be.'

Aside from the cares of his public life, Cardinal Gray relaxed with his favourite leisure time activity – DIY. Recently he had been engaged in restoring the handmade parquet floor in his domestic chapel at St Bennet's and in installing stained-glass windows.

Preparing for his trip to Rome, he observed, 'My regalia has to be bought in Rome. After all, that sort of outfit is just not to be had anywhere along Edinburgh's High Street!'

Late in April, the Cardinal-designate flew to Rome to attend a week-long meeting of the Congregation for the Evangelisation of Peoples. He spent the hour before his flight south answering some of the 1,000 letters which had poured into St Bennet's from all over the world since the announcement from Rome was made.

In Rome an embarrassing incident occurred. The Cardinal had to attend an important meeting at the Vatican and was waiting (in resplendent cardinal red ceremonial garb) for transport to arrive. It didn't ... and no taxis were available.

Fortunately a new student at the Scots College (where he was staying) had brought with his luggage a tiny Triumph TR7 sports car – bright blue, with shining chrome. In desperation, the Cardinal squeezed into the front seat of the trendy vehicle, feeling not a little awkward as they sped through the streets of Rome with an Italian police escort.

They arrived at the Vatican and the escort ceremoniously waved their hands. But another hand was raised – that of a bold gendarme!

Behind him, two Swiss Guards blocked the entry. Those halberds might well have stopped the two Scots if they had pierced the tyres of their tiny chariot!

But then – the *cardinatial* red was noticed! The surprise on their faces gradually gave way to concealed amusement and then back again to protocol. The gendarme bowed and waved them on. The Swiss Guards clicked heels, came to attention and gave them a dignified salute.

'I wanted to laugh,' admitted the Cardinal later, 'but there wasn't room. They wanted to laugh, but it just isn't done in the best Vatican circles. I have no doubt, though,' he continued, 'that the story of the undignified entry of the Scottish Cardinal to the Vatican City provoked some mirth when it was related afterwards in the canteen.'

A week later, on 29th April, some 422 Scottish Catholics also flew to Rome to be at the new Cardinal's side and to attend, not only his elevation to the purple (as Cardinal Priest of the title *Santa Chiara a Vigna Clara* – Rome's newest church), but a reception at the Scots College.

When they reached the piazza of St Peter's, the Scots party created a stir as they assembled in the centre and marched into the basilica with Archbishop Scanlan, a piper, and two banners (the St Andrew's saltire cross and the thistle) at their head. The piper was Pipe-Major Ronald Lawrie of Glasgow City Police Pipe Band, who had been driven straight to the square from the airport.

Speaking in English, Pope Paul VI addressed the wildly enthusiastic national pilgrimage in St Peter's: 'Tell your friends at home of the Pope's love for Scotland.'

His Scottish Cardinal knew this only too well – as a young priest, Paul VI had stayed the night with the Passionist community at Drummohr, near Prestonpans in East Lothian. The Pope loved to tell Cardinal Gray how he had slept on a mattress just two feet wide and as hard as the floorboards.

Gordon Joseph could never forget the moment when, on the third day of the Consistory where he had been named a Cardinal, he was called to the Papal altar. Why? He didn't know – but everyone in the Papal entourage did.

When he nervously arrived, Pope Paul embraced him. The master of ceremonies approached with a large reliquary in his hands containing a relic of the skull of St Andrew. He gave it to Pope Paul, who held it out to the Scottish Cardinal and said, with a smile: 'Peter greets his brother, Andrew.'

'I still remember vividly that moment,' said the Cardinal. 'I felt I was in Peter's net; that, come what might, he would draw me safely to the heavenly shore.'

Today these relics of St Andrew are preserved in the St Andrew Shrine at St Mary's Cathedral, Broughton Place in Edinburgh. Shortly before his death, Cardinal Gray was spotted by the Cathedral administrator kneeling in prayer before the relics.

Comparisons with Scotland's first Cardinal, David Beaton, were soon made.

'The circumstances are slightly different,' pointed out Cardinal Gray. 'Beaton was Chancellor of Scotland, whereas, as far as I was concerned, when I was appointed Cardinal no one knew quite what a Cardinal was and what his jurisdiction consisted of. I had to spend many occasions explaining that a Cardinal had no authority – he was merely an adviser to the Pope, particularly about conditions in different countries, or when he called a meeting of Cardinals. Apart from that he was only used to elect a new Pope when there was a Conclave. From a diocesan point of view he had no jurisdiction or authority at all, unless he happened to be a bishop.'

Cardinal David Beaton, Gordon Gray's predecessor, was born

in Fife and educated, like Cardinal Gray, at the University of St Andrews. He went for further studies to Glasgow and then to Paris, where he studied canon law, becoming Bishop of Mirepoix and the Scottish *resident* at the French court. He acquired French citizenship and was employed as an ambassador. He sat in the Scottish Parliament and was made a Cardinal through the influence of the French court, before being appointed Archbishop of St Andrews. In great measure, therefore, Beaton was a francophile ecclesiastic, born of the old *entente cordiale.*

Nominating Beaton as Archbishop of St Andrews had threatened the delicate relationship between St Andrews and Glasgow, which, from time to time, took the form of jousting for power between the two Sees – a tension which, over the following centuries and up to the present day, continued to be a significant characteristic of the Catholic Church in Scotland.

David Beaton became Regent of Scotland after the death of James V, and Chancellor of the Kingdom in 1543. His career, therefore, was at the heart of government at a time when Roman Catholicism was the established religion.

'He was without a doubt, very much a Scottish patriot,' adds Cardinal Gray, 'and was really one of the great minds in the country, quite apart from his role as a churchman.

'When I was made a Cardinal – after the official decree had been brought to the groups of Cardinals, I happened to be the senior one of my group of about 15. The Vatican Secretary of State presented us with the document from the Holy Father, saying we'd been appointed Cardinals of Honour. He had to read this document and I had to reply in Latin for the rest, which was rather amusing as I'd put it into Latin in the car going down. My Latin wasn't very good. The Latin of Canon Daniel Boyle, Rector of the Scots College, was *very* good.

'I sat in the car taking it down in Latin. After that we were each allotted a room to receive visitors of courtesy whom the embassies had sent to greet each new Cardinal and to sign their visitors book.

'There was one visitor who came, possibly an assistant to the Ministry to the Holy See. He wasn't a Beaton, but had ancestors from around that time in the government of the day, closely allied with John Knox. He came forward to me and said, "Congratulations, Your Eminence. You know, you'll be interested that one of my ancestors was one of the ones who used a dagger to pierce the heart of your predecessor, Cardinal Beaton." So I said "Let's forget the past".'

Back in Edinburgh again, Cardinal Gordon Joseph Gray attended a dinner on 14th May, hosted by the Scottish Bishops in his honour at the Caledonian Hotel. Among the 200 guests was Secretary of State, Willie Ross, who said:

'This is one of the most honourable national occasions it has been my privilege to attend. I felt it my duty to attend. I had to be here.

'It is a unique occasion to have a Scot elevated to this considerably responsible position in the Catholic Church.'

Other guests included the Lord Provost of Edinburgh, James McKay; the Moderator of the General Assembly of the Church of Scotland, Dr James Longmuir; the Primus of the Episcopal Church in Scotland, the Most Revd F H Moncrieff; Lord Clyde, President of the Court of Session; the Earl of Haddington and the Lieutenant-General, Sir Derek Lang.

In the early 1970s, the Cardinal continued to be heavily involved in the International Commission for English in the Liturgy (ICEL). Work was being done on adopting uniform texts for all prayers and acclamations said by the congregation at Mass; a Breviary for use in English-speaking countries and a Psalter were also under consideration. Finally, chants for the liturgical texts were a particular difficulty, because of the cultural differences among English-speaking countries.

Even as a Cardinal, Gordon Joseph had all too brief vacation time when he and two brother bishops – Bishop Colin Macpherson (Argyll and the Isles) and Bishop Stephen McGill (Paisley) took to the water for fishing holidays. Some of their favourite fishing lochs were near Oban where they fished for trout. On other occasions they would head out to South Uist – to West Bee, West Ollay or Loch West Olivat. Happy days in the rocking boat, picnics on the water and the smell of the sea!

CHAPTER 11

Committees and Commitment

ONE of the immediate pressures on the new Cardinal was the clamour from radical Catholics for change. Questioned in the autumn of 1969 by the Divine Word Missionary, Brother Paul, on the alleged 'autocratic exercise of authority in the Church in Scotland,' the Cardinal answered: 'Who is the Scottish Catholic Renewal Movement? I don't know. I don't remember ever having seen their membership given, either by name or by number. They're a very small, a very unimportant group. And if they feel the Church is autocratic in Scotland, they must be wearing glasses made of some kind of material that I personally have never come across.'

The Scottish Catholic Renewal Movement, based in Glasgow, came to the notice of the general public in the wake of lay protest at the encyclical *Humanae Vitae*. Its aim was to encourage intelligent debate on the problems facing Christians and to form public opinion in the Church.

Active as early as 1967, the SCRM had recently held a teach-in at the McLellan Galleries on the subject of 'Authority and Conscience – Crisis in the Church,' led by Norman St John-Stevas MP and Father Enda McDonagh of St Patrick's College, Maynooth. In subsequent meetings they were to invite the Jesuit theologian, Karl Rahner, to speak on 'The Democratisation of the Catholic Church' (1971); Professor Hans Küng (1971), Bernard Häring (1972), and the anti-Vietnam War Jesuit, Father Daniel Berrigan (1974). During those years, the SCRM made Glasgow an international centre for theological debate.

On 6th March 1970 there came a hard blow for the Cardinal to bear. His mother, aged 87, died. He conducted the funeral service on this especially sad occasion, losing one very special person in his life and in that of his family.

The cares of office proved to be increasingly heavy as the years went on.

'The spiritual good of the diocese demanded help and I asked for an auxiliary,' recalls the Cardinal. 'Rome does not hurry, but on 24th April 1970, I had the privilege of ordaining Bishop James Monaghan as my Auxiliary.

'He had been my secretary for five years and my vicar general from 1958. He became a tower of strength, was trusted and welcomed by clergy, religious and laity alike. If he had a fault, it was his loyalty to me. I'm sure there were times when he should have disagreed with my decisions.'

For the first time in his life as a bishop, Gordon Joseph was invited to attend not only a number of functions on the occasion of the General Assembly of the Church of Scotland in May 1970, but also to spend a night at the Palace of Holyroodhouse as a guest of the Lord High Commissioner, who that year was the Labour Member of Parliament Margaret Herbison Privy Councillor, the first woman to hold the office of High Commissioner.

The Cardinal, although reluctant to exchange his familiar bed at St Bennet's for an unfamiliar one at Holyrood, felt obliged out of courtesy to accept this gracious and very ecumenical invitation. So he packed his bags and drove to the Palace for the appointed time – around four in the afternoon.

Then, with the other guests, he attended a reception, mingling with those others who were not to be house guests. The latter (about 150 in number) left and the Cardinal, with the 20 guests remaining, sat down to dinner and then retired to the drawing-room for coffee, liqueurs and conversation.

During the course of the evening, the High Commissioner, whom the Cardinal found to be a charming person, beckoned him over to sit and converse with her.

Hardly had they finished taking coffee, when an aide (one of the officers on duty from the Forces) came and asked Her Grace if Cardinal Gray might be excused as there was a phone call for him from the Vatican! Naturally, she consented.

'The eyes of dear old Harry Whitley, minister of St Giles,'

recalled the Cardinal, 'a good friend despite our theological dis-agreements, his eyes gleamed in anticipation of what a Vatican phone call might entail, and he said "I'll come with you". Did his eyes twinkle – I don't know?'

The Cardinal and Dr Whitley were led down to the phone in the basement of the Palace. Who could it be? The voice at the other end replied 'Agnellus'. It was Agnellus Andrew, director of the Catholic Radio and Television Centre at Hatch End.

It transpired that Archbishop O'Connor had phoned St Bennet's and the Sisters had told him that he could not contact the Cardinal as he was at Holyrood.

The Archbishop had already written to the Cardinal a week or two before requesting that, as senior Cardinal on the Commission for Social Communications, he should chair the meetings.

The Cardinal had replied that he could not. His Italian was nil, he wrote; his Latin bad and his English not very good!

However, Father Agnellus, a fellow Scot, phoned to the effect that if he would agree to chair the Commission, the Vatican had agreed to install simultaneous translation. So that was that. He didn't tell Harry Whitley what the phone conversation was all about. He was sure Dr Whitley would have a sleepless night – wondering.

There was another occasion when Dr Whitley and the Cardinal sparred humorously. The two men shared the same tobacconist shop on George IV Bridge, not far from St Giles.

Habitually, they would discuss the merits of different blends of tobacco.

'One day,' recalled the Cardinal, 'I went into the shop and found that he had left me a small package. I opened it and found it was an ounce of *Presbyterian Mixture*.'

A few days later, Dr Whitley entered to the shop and was handed a parcel left for him by Cardinal Gray. He unwrapped it and discovered that it was a return present – a bottle of *VAT 69*!

In June 1970 the Cardinal was made a Fellow of the Educational Institute of Scotland at a ceremony in the Assembly Hall. The EIS (the oldest trade union in Scotland) had placed this citation on his diploma of Fellowship: ' … he having in his work and in his person exemplified the qualities of a great teacher by his selfless devotion to the future welfare of all those in his care, his recognition of individual human worth, his respect for and quest after sound knowledge and traditional skill, his ability to initiate and inspire, his wealth of outlook and clear, penetrating vision of the world of tomorrow, and above all his love and concern for young people everywhere.'

When the Cardinal arrived in Rome for the first plenary session of the Commission, the members were informed that if they wished to make an intervention, they should book in each morning and submit their script. The purpose of the meeting was to finalise the latest draft of the Pastoral Instruction on Communications.

The Cardinal told Monsignor Andrzej Deskur that he could not conduct a useful meeting of that nature without debate and free discussion. So, he opened the meeting with a prayer and announced that, since they would be examining the document paragraph by paragraph, anyone who might wish to intervene should hold up his hand. The Cardinal promised that he would keep a note of those wishing to speak and that each would be given his chance to speak. He also asked that no one should speak for more than eight minutes, saying that they would be given a one-minute warning before the bell for the end of their intervention.

This request worked admirably. Everyone who wished to had an opportunity to speak. Thus all enjoyed real discussions and lively debate. Everyone seemed happy and at the end of the week's meetings in late October, the Cardinal was presented with a magnificent folio volume of reproductions of Vatican paintings by Raphael (1483-1520), autographed by members of the Commission.

A few weeks later, in Edinburgh, the Cardinal played host to the advisory board of the ICEL. Subsequently, eleven bishops came to Edinburgh to attend the Episcopal Board of ICEL, as a gesture of respect to the Cardinal (who was due to relinquish his post as Scottish delegate), for having helped to found ICEL and having also served for six years as its chairman.

Speaking in June 1971 at the golden jubilee of Archbishop Scanlan's ordination, the Cardinal outlined some of the difficulties facing a bishop:

'A babel of voices seeks to drown, to contradict, to dilute

the authoritative teaching of Christ in matters of doctrine and morality as expounded by the teaching Church. A rash of philosophers, atheist, humanist, communist and pseudo-Christian, seeks to destroy belief in the supernatural and in the spiritual. An underworld of anarchy seeks to undermine and disrupt the exercise of the divine authority given by Christ to the College of the Apostles with Peter, and to the episcopate of today with Paul.'

The pastoral concerns of the Cardinal included more concrete problems. During the late 1960s and '70s – a time when celibacy for priests was being attacked and authority questioned – there were many failures and losses of ordained priests.

'I blame no one – except the priests who opted out,' wrote the Cardinal later. 'For some reason, the urban areas suffered most. There was no pattern. We lost priests who had gone through the junior seminary; priests who had been late vocations; priests who had been educated at Drygrange, Rome, Spain, Wonersh, St Edmunds, Ware and Oscott. That is why today we are desperately short of priests – and of men suitable to be chosen as bishops. During those post-Vatican II years, a violent attack of *ecclesiastical measles* struck seminaries throughout the Catholic Church.'

The strain on the Cardinal of dealing with this considerable haemorrhage of the clergy was immense. He felt deeply what he described as 'the heart-breaking and all-too frequent occurrences of priests suddenly deserting their priesthood.

'At one time, priests in such a situation, suddenly disappeared. But, in the early 1970s, one got to suspect or learn of their probable impending lapse. One saw them frequently – talked, prayed and pleaded with them; emphasised their commitment at ordination for life. I would change them to different parishes away from their present problems; gave them leave of absence. All to no avail.

'Later, they would come and state categorically that their minds were made up and that there was no use trying to dissuade them.

'It was a traumatic period, when one had many sleepless and agonising nights and days. And always with the nagging question-mark: Is it my fault? Where have I failed? Only God knows the answer.'

CHAPTER 12

Death and Election

CARDINAL Gray continued to break new ecumenical ground. At morning service early in December 1970, he became the first Cardinal to preach in King's College Chapel, Aberdeen since the Reformation. In his sermon he challenged the Ecumenical movement in Scotland to go forward more confidently. He cautioned the capacity congregation of 500 people, that many saw 'simply a Church at prayer. On television they watch the services of the different traditions of worship or ecumenical songs of praise. They see a Church withdrawn, enclosed, taken up with its own private world.'

He urged the Church not to be so modest:

'It is not very good at selling itself and publicising its good works. The Church has to its credit really immense achievements in the service of humanity. If the Churches have done so much in their isolation from each other, how much more they could do in ecumenical co-operation. Not simply by praying together, but by working together. Christian co-operation begins where there is human need. It begins (though it does not end) at home.'

In 1976, Cardinal Gray joined Pope Paul VI at the canonisation ceremony in Rome of the Jesuit martyr John Ogilvie, hanged at Glasgow Cross in 1615 – Scotland's first canonised saint for more than seven centuries and born in Banffshire, where the Cardinal's family came from.

Bishop John Mone, present at the Gesù Church in Rome the day after the canonisation, remembers how the Cardinal 'gathered up the whole Scottish scene, the Scottish identity. He could sum up so well the feelings in a Scottish heart.'

As chairman for seven years of the International Commission

for English in the Liturgy (ICEL), Gordon Joseph was directly involved in the kind of changes which provoked the rebellion of Archbishop Lefebvre in France and Father Oswald Baker in England, against the abolition of the old Tridentine rite and the Mass in Latin.

Recent storms over the Tridentine Mass had focused public interest on the Catholic Church. The Cardinal, however, was in favour of a pastoral approach:

'I think in order that the new rite of Mass and the vernacular Mass might be introduced, it was necessary for a time to say that this is the only one, but I see no reason why, later, Rome should not allow the Tridentine Mass to be used once more. It is only my own surmise, but it seems to be a case for tolerance.'

The Cardinal could afford to be tolerant – an independent Gallup Poll published in March 1977 showed that only nine per cent of Scottish Catholics preferred the old Tridentine Mass, with zero per cent of that number saying they would boycott the new vernacular Mass.

Another ecumenical milestone took place towards the end of May 1977, when the Cardinal was invited to the General Assembly of the Church of Scotland. Speaking at the Assembly Hall before the Queen and Prince Philip, he thanked Moderator John R Gray for his welcome. It was the first time he had enjoyed 'the privilege of being present at that deeply devotional, solemn and impressive act of worship.'

Gordon Joseph underlined the importance that ecumenical progress had for him as leader of the Roman Catholic Church in Scotland:

'I look back over the years of growth, years of discovery in the ways of reconciliation. It is true that formidable obstacles remain, but at least in these recent years we have learned how much we share in common.

'Before, we seemed to spend so much time on the differences, but now we have realised that we have one Faith, one Baptism, one Lord. The same Baptism, the same Sacred Scriptures now, thank God, available in an edition that we all accept. We have the same conviction of the power of prayer, the same love for the person of Christ and the same dedication to his service.'

Cardinal Gray had recently given his imprimatur to a new edition of the Revised Standard Version of the Bible. Originally prepared by non-Catholic biblical scholars in America, its production was handed over to the Catholic Church and, as it was printed in Edinburgh, Cardinal Gray was able to sanction it officially.

Commenting later on the Report of the Panel on Doctrine, the Revd Bernard Citron of Kirkcaldy said some of the differences between the Church of Scotland and the Roman Catholic Church were outdated and that the Bible played a far greater part in Roman Catholic teaching today than did tradition.

'We are becoming closer together and I wish we would study the Bible together. While in theory and dogma, the Roman Catholic Church is not changing its position about one Church, in practice, very much so, to get a Cardinal to come to this General Assembly and give it a very evangelical message is a sign, one of many signs, of recognition.'

The Grand Master of the Grand Orange Lodge of Scotland, Thomas Orr, criticised the Panel on Doctrine's statement, saying that it took 12,000 words and verbal gymnastics to indicate the obvious major doctrinal differences.

But the pressures of office had already exerted themselves on Cardinal Gray. In mid-July 1977, the Cardinal was due to lead the archdiocesan pilgrimage to Lourdes, but had to withdraw on doctor's orders. He was found to be suffering from exhaustion after several years of incessant activity with no significant breaks. He was ordered to rest for three months.

For some years he had been longing for a little remote cottage in the country where he could find seclusion – for peace, rest and quiet to prepare addresses and talks, to read and think – a refuge without the intrusion of a telephone. His health was then still reasonably good and he was more than capable of looking after himself and cooking his own meals.

It was then that a fervent and dedicated convert, Jock Home Robertson, offered him the use of a little apartment in his own home, Paxton House in Berwickshire. It was to Paxton, then, that Cardinal Gray came occasionally for a period of some two years in the late 1950s, living behind the little chapel where he could celebrate Mass daily. But, gradually, the two-hour drive from Edinburgh tired him. So, after two years, he reluctantly gave up the arrangement.

Then, by chance, he discovered a roofless cottage at Castle Moffat on the estate of Nunraw Abbey in a row of what had been farm-workers' homes. The ruin he had his eye on had been the shepherd's cottage, but it had caught fire and the roof was destroyed.

The Abbot of Nunraw kindly let him have it. With the help of the Abbey mason and joiner, it was eventually rebuilt to meet the Cardinal's requirements.

They dispensed with the attic floor and the dormer windows and provided a sitting-room with kitchenette, a small bedroom and a bathroom. It was quite adequate for his needs and could be warmed quickly with electric radiators and a hot water cylinder.

It was a wonderful refuge. Next door were two very friendly Italians who rented a cottage, but rarely stayed in it. As for the other two cottages – one was in a bad state of repair, and the other was occupied for a period of some three years by Father Hugh, a Cistercian monk from Nunraw, who had chosen to live there as a hermit.

Cardinal Gray had given him permission to *reserve* (keep) the Blessed Sacrament in his little chapel and, while he was in residence next door, he used to celebrate Mass with his hermit neighbour. On Sundays, Father Hugh would join his community for the principal Mass at Nunraw. On Wednesdays he would make his way again down to the Abbey.

Father Hugh Randolph spent his days in prayer and study, broken only by bouts of assembling little bottle-stoppers in the shape of tartan-clad Highlanders. These and other curios were supplied to local traders who sold them to tourists as souvenirs.

One dark and misty night, the Cardinal was approaching his hideout when he was brought up short by the sight of a figure in a white Cistercian habit, floating above the window near Father Hugh's front door, its arms swinging wildly in the breeze.

A cold fear seized the Cardinal as the figure drew slowly nearer and nearer – and then he suddenly realised it was Father

Hugh's white habit which he had washed and hung out to dry before retiring to bed. It was the only ghost the Cardinal had ever seen!

The cottage at Castle Moffat was such a complete refuge that in the night he could hear the thunder of silence. He loved it.

Thunder of a different kind accompanied a fervent message of support for the Pope written by Cardinal Gray in March 1978. On behalf of the Scottish Bishops he declared that they would always walk *with* the Pope, neither before nor behind – 'our theological position is simple; our philosophy is clear, our position is unassailable.' This statement was at the very heart of the Cardinal's episcopate.

In the summer of 1978, after a very heavy year, the Cardinal decided to enjoy a holiday alone – free to do as he pleased, to walk the lovely Lammermuir Hills, or to take a car and revisit the little fishing villages and towns along the coast from Dunbar nearly to Berwick.

He went down to the cottage on the Sunday morning of 6th August, after offering Mass at St Bennet's. The Sisters followed in their car with provisions for the week on his own.

They were having their lunch together when the clouds closed in and the rain began to fall. Heavier and heavier with the rain, the mist rolled down the slopes of the hills.

He decided that the Sisters must forgo their high tea and saw them off home before the mist turned to murky darkness.

Alone, the Cardinal completed his household chores, drew the curtains, finished saying the prayers of his Office, and sat down to relax. It was the Feast of the Transfiguration.

Just before nine o'clock he switched on the radio. The first news item said that Pope Paul VI had died after weeks of illness. Almost simultaneously the doorbell rang and his new neighbour (Father Hugh had been recalled to the Abbey to serve as Prior) told him that the BBC was on the telephone asking for a comment on the Holy Father's deteriorating state of health.

The Cardinal went next door and told the caller that His Holiness had just died. At once, he was asked to come to the Edinburgh studio right away to pay a tribute to the Pope to be used for the midnight and morning news broadcast.

The fog was thick. He said he could not drive home that night. They asked to come down to record a tribute. He agreed, gave them directions and promised to keep the lights in the cottage on.

They arrived around midnight. He welcomed them in and brewed some tea. Having recorded his statement, he promised to return to St Bennet's early in the morning.

He didn't get to bed that night. He felt shattered. He put his luggage and food into the car, locked up the cottage and was back at St Bennet's by six in the morning, to hear the phone ringing as he entered the house. It was Radio Forth, wanting a tribute over the phone for the seven o'clock news.

He took part in two television programmes that morning – for the BBC and for Scottish Television. Although by then there was a Catholic Press Office, he had to answer dozens of calls from the press.

Then he sat down to think and plan, to cancel engagements for the rest of the month and prepare to leave for Rome, with no idea of when he would be free to return home.

He only knew that he wanted to be present at Pope Paul's Requiem and interment. Then, as a Cardinal he would be obliged to remain for the unknown experience of a *conclave* and the installation of a new Pope. He was sad, confused and very tired.

* * *

Cardinal Gordon Joseph spent three or four days tidying up his desk and cancelling engagements. Packing. He needed light clothes and he might be away for weeks or months. Who could guess? He packed a heavy case, ready for all eventualities, and left for Rome.

It was a cloudy, dull day when the Cardinal left St Bennet's for Turnhouse airport. There he was met by several press photographers and a television camera. He checked in his luggage for Rome and caught the shuttle for London.

After a long wait in London he boarded the Boeing 747 for Rome. It was a cramped and uncomfortable flight and was almost an hour late in taking off. His miserable meal was made worse as there was no room to manoeuvre the plastic knife and fork!

Once in Rome, there was another long delay before his luggage arrived. He couldn't find a trolley and had to haul three cases across the airport. It was the worst journey to Rome he had ever made.

Outside there was glorious sunshine, a cloudless sky and just enough breeze to make the heat bearable. As he settled into his rooms in the Scots College, the Cardinal wondered how long he would have to stay. At least a month, he told himself.

On the morning of 10th August, he discovered that there was to be a General Congregation of Cardinals at 11 o'clock in the Apostolic Palace. He left the Scots College just before 10 a.m. and went straight to St Peter's to say a prayer at the body of the Holy Father as it lay in state.

The coffin was a wedge-shaped casket sloping down from the head. He looked peaceful and truly at rest. 'He had changed little since we last saw him in March,' recalled the Cardinal.

Now the crowds were moving quietly, prayerfully, many in tears. The procession of people who had come to pay their last respects went on each day from when the basilica was opened until nightfall.

Four Swiss Guards stood at each corner of the coffin and the lighted Paschal Candle, symbolising the Resurrection, was placed behind the coffin head.

'It was a moving and memorable occasion I will never forget,' wrote the Cardinal to the Ursuline nuns back in Edinburgh.

At the Apostolic Palace about forty Cardinals assembled at the Congregation. The new arrivals took the oath of secrecy and business proceeded until shortly after 1.00 p.m. Most of it was conducted in Italian, some in Latin. During the vacancy, the authority of most of the Curia lapses and it was necessary to hold a Congregation each day to allow the College of Cardinals to make the decisions of Church government. These meetings were chaired by the *Camerlengo* (temporary chairman), Cardinal Jean Villot, assisted by the 80-year old Cardinal Confalonieri, Dean of the College of Cardinals.

Cardinal Gray returned to the Scots College for lunch, followed by a siesta – which was interrupted by a short thunder storm. Father Agnellus Andrew arrived in the evening to prepare for his commentary on the funeral of the Holy Father. He and the Cardinal talked until almost midnight.

Early the next day the Cardinal went to Gammarelli, the clerical tailors, and was measured for a very light piped soutane without a cape. The heat in Rome was humid and overpowering. He had to get something very light, with the prospect of weeks of meetings in unventilated rooms.

At the Congregation there were about sixty Cardinals present. Arrangements were made for the Mass on the steps of St Peter's and the Cardinals were briefed for that by the Master of Ceremonies, Monsignor Noé.

Cardinal Gray sat beside Cardinal Bertoli, who spoke good English and had been very kind and friendly to his Scottish colleague, giving him the gist of the discussions when the language problem left him at sea – he wished the other Cardinals would speak slowly, especially when using Italian. Security was tight. The Cardinal had a police escort to the meetings. The police also kept an eye on the Scots College by day and night.

At 11 o'clock the following morning, Saturday 12th August, the College of Cardinals assembled in the Consistorial Hall to meet the Diplomatic Corps. The Dean of the Corps, the Guatemalan ambassador, read an address of sympathy and Cardinal Confalonieri replied on behalf of the Cardinals. 'It was a very formal and sombre occasion,' wrote the Cardinal.

After lunch and a short siesta, the Cardinal vested in choir dress and left for the funeral at St Peter's. After a last farewell to Pope Paul, still lying in state, with the coffin not yet closed, they went to the Chapel of St Sebastian, just beside the Pietà, Michelangelo's acclaimed statue, and vested for Mass.

It was a magnificent setting and the Piazza was black with the crowd of mourners. 'I thought the unrehearsed ceremony went off with great dignity, beauty and solemnity,' commented the Cardinal, 'although rather on the long side.'

At the end of the absolutions, the Cardinals processed into St Peter's and lined up the length of the basilica as the body was carried in and down to the crypt to be enclosed in a lead shell and an oak outer casket. One of the most moving moments was when the Cardinals heard the bursts of clapping swelling louder and louder as the procession approached the great doors of St Peter's. Only half a dozen Cardinals, the Papal household and the Holy Father's relatives and personal friends were allowed down to the crypt.

'The Papacy must have caused Paul VI great suffering,' wrote the Cardinal, 'not only in the aftermath of Vatican II and the sometimes unpopular decisions he had to make and which brought him criticism and abuse, but (as his last will and testament shows) in the personal loneliness and separation from his family. He could never return to Brescia, nor to his diocese of Milan. His last will and testament shows how much that cost him.

'From the moment of his election, Paul had to give up home and family and enter his apartments in the Vatican, knowing that he would no longer be free to go where he wanted to, or even plan his own life. Never to return to Milan – even to walk through the house where he lived, or say goodbye to his friends. Never again choose how to spend a holiday. Paul's fifteen years as Pope were fifteen years of slavery – always subject to the beck and call of others.'

After unvesting, Archbishop Winning, Bishop Thomson and the Cardinal went for a dinner at the home of the Minister to the Holy See. The Duke of Norfolk (representing the Queen), and Mervyn Rees of the Home Office (representing the Government), were present, as well as Lord Ramsay (the former Archbishop of Canterbury), Cardinal Hume and the Archbishops of Birmingham and Liverpool. They finished at midnight and returned home through the deserted streets of Rome. It was the beginning of the Roman holiday and the city was very empty. Shops and restaurants were closed and the traffic lights switched off.

Next day, a Sunday, was a quiet day. After concelebrating Mass, the Cardinal had to go to the Vatican. Each Cardinal met the official delegation representing his own country. The King and Queen of Spain were present, as well as Mrs Carter (wife of the American President), the Duke of Norfolk and some two hundred others. After the speeches, the guests mingled with the Cardinals. Cardinal Gray found the heat in the Sala Ducale unbearable and left as soon as it was decently possible.

That evening at six o'clock another Mass was concelebrated

by fifty of the Cardinals in front of a very large congregation. After Mass, the Cardinals processed out of St Peter's and into the crypt where they recited prayers beside the tomb of Paul VI.

The tomb was surmounted by a large slab of brown marble, slightly wedge-shaped. The inscription in red letters was simply - *Paulus VI PP.* The coffin had been buried, as Paul himself wished, in the earth far below, in Scarvae, an early burial ground excavated below St Peter's some years before and unquestionably the burial place of Saint Peter.

'It is a wonderful place,' wrote the Cardinal, full of chapels and tombs still bright with the mosaics and paintings of two thousand years ago.'

The next day, in the presence of the Cardinals and a huge congregation, the first of a *novendiales* (nine days prayer) of Masses was celebrated in St Peter's for the repose of his soul.

Each morning the Cardinals assembled to discuss and decide on urgent matters involving the everyday business of the Church. Each evening the Cardinals gathered at St Peter's for the *novendiales* Mass.

The date for the Conclave was fixed for 25th August. In the morning, the Mass for the election of a Pope was celebrated in St Peter's before the altar of the throne, with Cardinal Villot as celebrant. He preached a short homily.

On the previous morning, at the meeting of the Cardinals, the cells had been allotted by ballot. After Mass on 25th August, all the Cardinals were free to find their accommodation and bring in their luggage.

At 4.30 p.m. in the afternoon they assembled in the Pauline Chapel in choir-dress before processing into the Sistine Chapel, preceded by the Sistine Chapel choir which led the singing of the *Veni Creator* (Come, Creator Spirit) and by Monsignor Virgilio Noé, the master of ceremonies, with a number of assistants.

The Cardinals entered the Sistine Chapel *seniores priores* (oldest first) and found their tables along each side of the Chapel walls – just a chair, a narrow table, a splendid red blotting-pad, a pen and voting-cards for the session scheduled to begin next day.

Then Monsignor Noé cried out: *'Exeant omnes!'* (Everyone leave!) and all except the Cardinals left the Chapel. The great doors were closed with a liturgical clatter, the key was turned in the massive lock and the Conclave began.

One hundred and eleven Cardinals remained, all new to a Conclave (except perhaps ten, who had been present in 1963 when Pope Paul VI was elected), all silently wondering what the coming days or weeks might bring ....

'Actually, that first gathering was rather dull and formal,' recalled Cardinal Gray later. Paul VI had in 1975 anticipated the Conclave that would follow his death, and had updated and modified the constitution *Romano pontifice eligendo*, outlining in detail the procedure to be followed.

It required an oath sworn by each Cardinal that he would observe secrecy concerning all that would take place during the Conclave, and that anyone who might introduce technical instruments for recording or transmitting the happenings of the Conclave would be immediately expelled.

When the session was over, the times for concelebrated Masses were arranged and the Cardinals were free. Gordon Joseph made his way to his cell where he would spend the night. Although the Vatican was not built as a 5-star hotel, he was fortunate. His accommodation was in a large partitioned office on the mezzanine floor. It was a big office which had been divided into two areas by a six-foot high unpainted and fresh three-ply partition. Each half had its own door, but only one switch for the electric light.

He discussed the situation with his stable-companion – an old friend who spoke perfect English. They decided that 'lights out' would be around half ten. He had the switch.

Half of Gordon Joseph's apartment was stacked high with tables, chairs and typewriters. His living quarters were furnished with a small chair and a wooden table on which lay some blank sheets of paper, a ball-point pen, a table lamp, a bottle of mineral water and a glass. In the opposite corner was a hospital bed, a small bedside table with a flash lamp, a ewer of water, a basin, a towel and some soap. There was also a strip of carpet at the bedside – about four by two feet.

He and his brother Cardinal were fortunate, for ten yards away was a large cloakroom with a wash-hand basin and toilets.

He settled in and in due course descended the stairs to the

dining-room for supper. It was a good simple Italian meal without frills and with the customary glass of wine. It was a quiet and subdued meal and the Cardinals drifted out when they wished.

Gordon Joseph made his way back to his quarters.

'I am not sure when I experienced my Road to Damascus,' remembered the Cardinal. 'Was it evening or in the light of the morning? Silence seemed to reign throughout the Vatican as I made my way to my room. I stopped in the wide corridor with its splendid murals. I suddenly felt alone in the vast building. The windows were obscured with white paint. They were closed and guarded with a chain and leaden seals. Somewhere there were 111 Cardinals, each engaged in his own thoughts. No radio, no telephone, no newspapers. Just silence – cut off from the world as I had never been before. Yet, not alone. I felt the unseen Presence of the Holy Spirit. I knew I was not alone. He was there to guide me, to guide *us*, despite our human failings; there to be with us and direct us in fulfilling the Divine Will. I went to my room and prayed – *Sanctus Spiritus Subveniet* (The Holy Spirit will help). Throughout that Conclave I lived in His Presence.'

On the morning when the voting began, the Cardinals celebrated Mass, had their breakfast of coffee and bread, and then made their way to the Sistine Chapel. They passed the iron stove on the left of the entrance-doors, the stove in which the voting-cards would be burnt until an election was completed. Its long chimney would then belch out white smoke to announce to the waiting crowds that '*Habemus Papam!*' (We have a Pope!).

'Journalists have speculated on the events of that historic day,' wrote Cardinal Gray. 'All I can say is that my greatest and most awesome moment was when my time in the procession of Cardinals arrived and, holding my voting-card in my hand before sliding it into the chalice-like receptacle on the altar, I, almost trembling, uttered my oath: "I call to witness Christ the Lord, who will be my judge, that my vote is given to the one whom before God I consider should be elected".

'The gossips in newspapers, journals and best-sellers have spoken of plots, pacts and intrigues; of secret meetings by day and by night.

'I can only say that no one who voiced that solemn and frightening oath could have anything but a clear and peaceful conscience and a conviction that his will was to do God's will.

'Eventually the stove, filled with ballot-papers (and the chemical which was added to emit white smoke), was ignited around 6.30 p.m. The stove misbehaved and, in the fading light, the smoke was neither black nor white, but greyish in colour.

'But, at 7.15 p.m., Vatican Radio announced on its loudspeakers that it was indeed definitely white. Minutes later, Cardinal Pericle Felici appeared on the balcony of St Peter's to announce to the multitude and to the world: "*Annuntio vobis gaudium magnum – Habemus Papam Albinum Luciani qui sibi imposuit nomen Johannem Paulum Primum*" (I announce a great joy to you – we have a Pope, Albinus Luciani, who has taken the name of John Paul the First).

'A little later Pope John Paul I appeared on the balcony to the cheering crowds. He wore a white soutane and gave his first Papal Blessing. Supper that evening was a great and joyful *festa*.'

CHAPTER 13

The Second Conclave

GORDON Joseph only met Pope John Paul I on three occasions. The first was on the day of his election, when they chanced to meet on the way downstairs. The Pope's French was good enough, Gordon Joseph's was bad. John Paul's English was, however, very poor, but they managed to chat and, as they were both pastoral bishops, the Pope found much in common with the Scottish Cardinal.

The second time was when the Cardinals lined up to offer their congratulations – if that is the right word for one elected to the frightening office of Pope, Vicar of Christ – when he addressed his College of Cardinals in the Sistine Chapel after a sleepless night.

There was a third occasion when, after his public inauguration Mass in front of St Peter's, Gordon Joseph again knelt to kiss his hand.

'Apart from these times, I only saw him on the television screen,' remembered Cardinal Gray later. 'How I admired him – so human. Like myself, he could not keep his *zucchetta* (skull-cap) straight, and he seemed to love bringing children from the crowd up to himself and quizzing them on their educational knowledge. Here was a different Pope. A Pope for the people. A very human Pope, who could relate to all of us.'

Cardinal Gray returned to Edinburgh to continue his pastoral engagements. His work was done. The Church had a Pope. It was in good hands. Long might he reign.

'Some might not have agreed,' added Cardinal Gray. 'We, the pastoral bishops, certainly did.'

It wasn't for long. In a short time John Paul achieved a great deal. He changed the papacy. He was a bridge from the old to the new.

'I can say from my heart,' added Cardinal Gray, 'that John Paul II could not have done what he has done – become an apostle to the world, an outgoing evangelising pilgrim – except for the short but quietly revolutionary thirty-three days of the reign of John Paul I (a day for each year in the life of Christ).'

Cardinal Gray was happily at home getting on with his pastoral visits to parishes, religious communities and schools, when the shattering news came over the radio. John Paul had been found in bed, with his bedside light on. He was dead. It was the morning of Friday 29th September 1978. The doctors agreed that he had died several hours before from a massive heart-attack.

The press had a field day. Had he been murdered? Had he been considered inadequate for his office and been quietly taken away? Why no post mortem?

For the Cardinals, about to make up for lost time in their pastoral responsibilities, the death brought problems as well as shock. Another absence from home. Cardinal Gray returned to Rome on 1st October and prayed before the body of the Pope as it lay in state at St Peter's.

The media prophets, of course – long before four o'clock on Wednesday 4th October when the Cardinals, diplomats and the multitude of mourners took their damp chairs or stances in front of St Peter's for the funeral of a unique but somewhat enigmatic Pope – the prophets and the press were already drawing up the odds on the results of the next Conclave, which was scheduled to start on 14th October.

Every word a Cardinal uttered in public was assessed and he was given his place among the 'runners' accordingly. Everyone who preached at the Novendiales Masses was assumed to have offered a tip to adjust the odds. Ladbrokes could have suffered large losses if they had read and accepted the superior tipsters of *The Times* and *The Guardian*.

Cardinal Gray was in a happy position. Even the Scottish daily papers did not include him in its list of *papabiles* (possible Popes).

One hundred and eleven Cardinals were to elect the new Pope. Oaths of secrecy were taken once more and Saturday 21st October was announced for the Mass of the Election of a Pope and their entry into the Conclave.

He was fortunate in the ballot for cells and found himself allotted a very comfortable little room with a bathroom next door. There was less paint covering the windows and, though the temperature was cooler than in August and September, some of the windows could be opened.

Now the Cardinals were no longer strangers; the atmosphere was more relaxed. They knew the ropes and the procedure that would be followed.

Gordon Joseph was not a silent observer at the Conclaves. Not only did he know many of the Cardinals, but he studied the *curriculum vitae* of each. He considered their age, experience and reputation among their peers. He prayed a lot before the time came to vote. As a complete and happy outsider, he could take a very objective view of the field.

It was not until the Monday evening that the white smoke obediently (and with no ambiguity as to its colour) spiralled out of the chimney above the stove in the Sistine Chapel. The cheering and applause resounded throughout St Peter's Square. It was not until 6.44 p.m. that the secret was out, when Cardinal Felici appeared on the balcony and announced again '*Annuntio vobis gaudium magnum*'.

He delayed for a moment before divulging that the Cardinals had surprised the world – a non-Italian, after 455 years, and, moreover, a Pope from Communist-dominated Poland. A surprise indeed.

The second Conclave had gone into a second day. Many writers have told their story of the Conclave – from outside.

'I can only say,' emphasised Cardinal Gray nine years later, 'that Cardinal Wotyla, Pope John Paul II, was elected by the Holy Spirit, his apostolate made possible by John Paul I, the Bridgemaker. I can say no more – except that immediately after his election, I ruined my nail-scissors! I cut through the chain that had closed the window of my cell, and I cut through its seal. Then I took it home for my collection of medals and mementoes to leave to my successor.

'I was happy with the outcome of the Conclave. I had known

Cardinal Wotyla for many years. I had admired him. I now loved him as my spiritual Father in God. Each day I pray many times for him.'

In February 1979 the Cardinal had the joy of promulgating a decree declaring *Venerable* the former factory girl and nun, Margaret Sinclair, also known as the 'Edinburgh Wonder Worker'.

Although by now his health was not good – he was walking with the aid of a stick – he accompanied Pope John Paul to Poland in June that year. The Cardinal later described it as 'a week of intense spiritual inspiration, of Christian gaiety and joy, in cities carpeted with flowers and echoing the music of song. A great nation subjected but never subdued – rejoiced in the Pope who had come back to say goodbye.

'As always in life, joy was tinged with sadness, especially in the airport at Cracow, when the plane carrying Pope John Paul II and his retinue disappeared into the distant skies.'

Then on to France at the end of May 1980 for a long weekend. Highlights of the visit were the open-air Mass at Le Bourget and the Pope's address to the United Nations.

Accompanying the Cardinal was Father Tony McNally, who had studied in France and knew Paris. He took the Cardinal in a taxi for a guided tour of the city and then for a magnificent meal in a hotel.

It was during this visit to France that Cardinal Thomas O'Fiach of Ireland turned to Cardinal Gray and urged: 'Gordon, you must bring the Pope to Scotland' – thus the seeds of the idea were sown.

Further academic honours then fell to the Cardinal. An honorary degree was conferred on him by Heriot-Watt University on 14th November 1981. In the Assembly Hall of the Church of Scotland, the Cardinal received his honorary doctorate along with the Edinburgh film-star, Sean Connery.

The year 1982 was to be the climax of Cardinal Gray's episcopate, for Pope John Paul II agreed to visit England, Wales, Ireland and Scotland. There was tremendous excitement in each of these countries and preparation of all kinds, involving large numbers of people from all sections of the Catholic Church.

But there were already darker clouds on the horizon – war against Argentina over the Falkland Islands had broken out.

War between nations was an increasingly controversial issue. The Scottish Bishops, including Cardinal Gray, had recently made a statement on nuclear war.

Privately the Cardinal noted that 'the statement from the Scottish Bishops on nuclear war was very carefully worded and was intended to be a document that might stir up discussion among so many of our people who do not want to be involved.

'Personally – but I could not say this nor involve my brother bishops in my own views – I feel almost convinced that unilateral disarmament is the only way in conformity with the teaching of Our Blessed Lord. But who am I to put forward a view? I would not dare to do so. The whole question of legitimate war is so complicated. And now we are standing on the threshold of what could escalate into even a Third World War with no greater motive than pride in sovereignty. I cannot write to the papers. I do not want to be quoted. That is one of the problems of being a bishop.'

When it was announced that the airstrip on Port Stanley had been bombed, Cardinal Gray protested. He issued a statement on 1st May 1982 that 'with the vast majority of my fellow countrymen, I am deeply distressed that the government is finding it necessary to give the go-ahead for the use of force in the Falklands dispute.'

On 28th May three telegrams of protest over the Papal visit were sent to the Queen, Prince Charles and the Prime Minister, Mrs Margaret Thatcher on behalf of the Religion and Morals Committee of the Free Presbyterian Church of Scotland. The telegrams were sent by the Revd John MacLeod of Stornoway, Clerk of the Committee.

In mid-May Cardinal Hume and Cardinal Gray were in Rome for desperate talks to try to avoid cancellation of the Pope's visit to Britain. After a few days the Cardinals returned to Britain. Cardinal Gray felt that it was hopeless.

The day after he returned home, Cardinal Gray telephoned Archbishop Winning to give him a full report on the current situation. The following day, the Archbishop sent telegrams to the heads of the main lay Catholic organisations in Scotland, asking them to telegraph the Holy Father, encouraging him to come.

He also contacted all the Scottish Bishops and secured their agreement to send a telegram from them all to the Pope, bearing an identical message. Telegrams were also sent to the two Argentinian Cardinals, urging them to encourage the Papal visit to Scotland, in spite of the hostilities.

On the Saturday came the reply from Archbishop Warlock, who indicated that he had been given clearance by Cardinal Basil Hume to go to Rome. The following day, Cardinal Gray asked Archbishop Winning to come over to Edinburgh and stay the night at St Bennet's. He arrived at midnight and the two men talked until morning. They decided that Archbishop Winning would also fly out to Rome.

When the two Archbishops – Winning and Warlock – met at Heathrow airport, it transpired that there was a go-slow on Italian airlines and things looked impossible until the Italian Embassy arranged for them to take a military plane. They finally flew out that afternoon, arriving at the Vatican in the evening.

The next day they met Cardinal Achille Silvestrini of the Secretariat of State and had lunch with the Pope, along with the Argentinian Archbishops, López Trujillo and Martinez, and Cardinal Agostino Casaroli. After lunch the British and Argentinian Archbishops got down to some hard discussion.

They all met the Pope the next day and he informed them that he wanted their respective Cardinals to be present. Archbishop Warlock contacted Cardinal Hume, while Archbishop Winning telephoned Cardinal Gray, passing on the Pope's request.

'Tom,' said Cardinal Gray, 'I'll do anything for the Pope. I'm on my way.' He dropped everything and got ready to travel to Rome.

At the same time, the two Argentinian Cardinals – Raul Primatesta and Juan Aramburu – set off for Rome for the discussions.

When all four Cardinals and the Archbishops from both sides finally met in Rome, the friendship which Bishop McGill and the Cardinal had enjoyed with the Argentinian Bishops at the Second Vatican Council in 1962, came to unexpected fruition in 1982.

'The first meeting on May 21st was to be at a working lunch,'

Cardinal Gray wrote later. 'Cardinal Hume and myself were waiting in an ante-room to the Papal apartment when they arrived. Shall I ever forget! Cardinal Aramburu entered the room. His eyes opened wide when he saw me and he came straight to me, embraced me and kept repeating "Bene, bene – Gordon!" I felt Vatican II was still bearing its fruit. A little bonus that helped in 1982.'

A formula was agreed to make it clear that the Papal visit to Britain was a *pastoral* one. Then there followed a Mass of Reconciliation in St Peter's on the Saturday morning, with all the Bishops and Cardinals joined in prayer.

Last words from Pope John Paul stated that it would be up to the two British heirarchies to tell him whether the visit was on or off. Before flying back to Scotland, Cardinal Gray commented that he was reasonably optimistic that the door to the visit taking place was not yet closed. The British Cardinals and Bishops returned home, realising that it was their responsibility to tell the Holy Father not to come if matters grew worse in the days to come.

Meanwhile, back in Scotland, preparations were getting well advanced for the Pope's arrival. A year before, the Very Revd Bill Johnston, then Moderator of the General Assembly, had been informed of the impending Papal visit by Cardinal Gray:

'The Papal visit was the climax of Gordon Gray's cardinalate and he was naturally anxious that everything should be carefully planned. He was equally anxious that no offence should be given to Protestant sentiments in Scotland.

'When the time came to make the detailed arrangements for the meeting of the Pope with the then Moderator,' Bill Johnston recalled, 'I was Convenor of the Church's Inter-Church Relations Committee which had the responsibility from the Church of Scotland side, a partnership which led us to have many meetings to discuss details of what was to be a historic occasion when for the first time in 400 years, Pope and Moderator would shake hands.'

However, the precise mechanics of that meeting at first defied solution. Bill Johnston again:

'Our first idea was that the Pope should visit the Moderator at his flat in Charlotte Square and be entertained to tea. But the Chief Constable vetoed that, by saying that he could not guarantee security for such a visit. So over many lunches we tried to think of other venues, until one day Gordon said to me: "Aren't you tired of thinking of places for the two to meet? Let's go down to the Chief Constable and talk it all out with him".'

The two churchmen went off to police headquarters at Fettes Avenue to tell the Chief Constable, John Orr, of their difficulties.

'We've thought of *everything*,' they said. 'We've even thought of the quadrangle of the Assembly Hall.'

At this, John Orr sat up and remarked, 'That would be quite perfect – I would have no security problem there.'

Bill Johnston reminded the Cardinal that it would mean the historic handshake taking place under the statue of John Knox, to which he replied, 'Where better?'

On 31st May, however, far off in the Falklands, battle raged for control of Mount Kent and other strategic high ground on the approaches to Port Stanley. It was announced that the Atlantic Conveyor, hit by an Exocet missile the previous week, had now sunk.

At 5.25 p.m., forty minutes late, on Tuesday 1st June, the British Caledonian BAC One-Eleven plane carrying Pope John Paul II touched down at RAF Turnhouse. Meeting him was Cardinal Gray, leader of Scotland's 837,000 Catholics. He went up the aircraft steps, greeted the Pope inside the plane and persuaded him to make an unexpected change in his custom of kissing the tarmac. Upon descending from the plane, the Pope went over to the grass verge, bent down and reverently kissed the soil of Scotland, the *filia specialis* (special daughter of the Holy See) so called from the Papal Bull of Pope Honorius, issued in 1216, a major turning-point in the history of the medieval Church as it asserted Scotland's independence from the jurisdiction of the Archbishop of York.

The Cardinal introduced the Pope to Tom Morgan, Lord Provost of Edinburgh, to Archbishop Winning and the eleven Scottish Bishops, all of whom were wearing security-classified identification cards with colour photographs on their chests.

George Younger, Secretary of State for Scotland and Air Vice-Marshal Tim Lloyd, Air Officer Scotland and Northern Ireland were withdrawn at the last minute, to avoid the possibility of having the Pope criticised for appearing to associate himself with British militarism. The servicemen in the crowd were ordered not to wear uniforms.

At half past five the Pope left Turnhouse, travelling by road to Murrayfield where 44,000 young Scots heard him. 'Young people of Scotland, I love you!' – an enormous shout of joy ... interrupted with cheering on more than 30 occasions ... 'John Paul! John Paul! He's got the whole world in his hands!' ... 'You'll never walk alone!' ... 'O Flower of Scotland!'

Then around ten to seven the Pope was driven from Murrayfield to St Mary's Cathedral. Halfway along Princes Street he turned up the Mound to the home of the General Assembly. Two hundred demonstrators, led by the Revd Ian Paisley near the Assembly Hall, were prevented by police from breaking through barriers.

Crowds on the Mound drowned out the jeers from the placard-waving demonstrators. On the steps leading into the Assembly Hall quadrangle, and in the shadow of the statue of John Knox, John Paul was greeted by the Moderator, the Right Revd Professor John McIntyre, by nine former Moderators and their wives.

Professor McIntyre told the Pope that the history of Scotland was scarred by many occasions of religious conflict and controversy:

'From the spirit of reconciliation which informs our meeting today we, for our part, look forward to further dialogue with your Church, not only on subjects of disagreement, but also on the joint themes on which we agree in the face of a hostile world.'

Among the people presented to the Pope was Professor James Mackey of the Thomas Chalmers Chair of Systematic Theology at New College, himself a laicised, former Roman Catholic priest.

In a brief meeting at seven o' clock the two men, Pope and Moderator, exchanged courtesies.

'I still treasure the moment on the steps of the Assembly Hall,' adds former Moderator Bill Johnston, 'when the Moderator and the Pope were shaking hands for the first time in 400 years. Gordon Gray turned to me and embraced me with a tremendous hug. It was a sign not just of personal friendship, but of all that he had done over the years to bridge the gap that separates church people from each other. And for that, he made a host of friends, not least in my own Church of Scotland.'

Then the Pope made his way back to Princes Street and St Mary's Cathedral, where he addressed 1,000 priests, nuns and monks who were cheering wildly and waving Papal flags. He left the Cathedral at half past eight to go to St Bennet's.

Early on Tuesday, leaders of Scotland's other denominations, including Professor McIntyre, Jewish and Islamic leaders, met at St Bennet's to join the Pope for discussions. The Pope spoke of working together for the promotion of human values and of his desire for full unity between Churches. He said the will for unity was a sign of hope to a divided world. During the meeting, the Moderator and the Pope exchanged gifts of a silver quaich and a silver statuette of the Good Shepherd.

At the press conference, Professor McIntyre, who was due to pay a courtesy visit to the Pope the following spring, praised John Paul as a man of peace and reconciliation who had re-drawn the character of the Papal office. 'We are looking to this meeting with a sense of expectation, that as a result the dialogue between Catholics and Protestants will be furthered.'

Responding to misgivings and protests over the meeting, Professor McIntyre said, 'I understand why people are unhappy about this meeting. They are understandably afraid that the things for which the martyrs died should be lost. But nobody has ceded an inch on these basic points so far.'

Tuesday also included a visit to St Joseph's Hospital, Rosewell and then to St Andrews College, Bearsden, before the Pope and the Scottish Bishops assembled for Mass at Bellahouston Park, Glasgow in sublime sunshine with thousands spread before them – a field full of folk enjoying the peace of prayer. Sharing the Eucharistic prayer with Pope John Paul, was Cardinal Gray: 'Remember now your people, especially those for whom we now pray. Remember all of us gathered here before you. You know how firmly we believe in you.' And The Battlefield Band played, as well as the brass instruments from Troy, and the be-ribboned Polish choir joined in the song of the huge congregation.

The Pope invited everyone to walk hand in hand with their Christian brothers and sisters of the Reformed Churches.

Then came the return from Bellahouston to Edinburgh. The helicopter which brought them from the West, circled in the sunshine round the two slopes of Salisbury Crags which were dotted with people.

'When we made our way from the helipad at Holyroodhouse into the "pope-mobile" after the Holy Father's glorious reception at Bellahouston,' recalled the Cardinal, 'the streets were thick with cheering crowds.

'The Pope opened the window and leant out, shaking hands with the crowd.

'We instructed the driver to turn the pope-mobile so that His Holiness could speak to the ever-gathering crowds of 15 to 20,000 who massed outside our temporary enclosure in the Park.

'Along the Queen's Park to Salisbury he passed, then into Grange Road. On both sides, flags, handkerchiefs, umbrellas, hats, waving in the glorious sunset. Smiling police, joyful on-lookers, all happiness and a truly Scottish welcome. And the smiling Holy Father, blessing to left and right as we made our way slowly to the temporary railings erected for the Papal visit and closing off the roads that passed St Bennet's.

'Arriving at St Bennet's, we were met by a cheering crowd of some 3,000 people. Archbishop Marcinkus and Chief Superintendent Ian McPherson had anticipated just such a reception. One of them handed the Holy Father a loud-hailer. He spoke to the crowd for just a couple of minutes. He thanked them for the reception they had given him, the love they had shown; told them they must be tired after waiting so long. Then he blessed them in Latin and wished them goodnight – "I wish you one thing: it is a good sleep".'

As he went into St Bennet's, the Pope summed up the day – 'It was wonderful.' The cheers went on for a long, long time, as the sun sank gently in a golden-red sunset.

'I was proud to be a citizen of this great capital,' wrote the Cardinal.

The crowds did not disperse. Hundreds of young folk camped out in sleeping-bags all night, so as to have a last glimpse of John

Paul II when he passed by in the morning, headed for Turnhouse airport.

The Pope's visit, the Cardinal explained, was only the beginning of what would be a renaissance for Catholics in Scotland. He had seen joy, enthusiasm and people proud to be Christian. The Catholic Church, which had been underdogs in Scottish society, which had had a chip on its shoulder and had only fairly recently had access to the professions or the higher areas of industrial and commercial life, now was entering a new era of liberation and confidence.

As for the fears of extremists that Catholics might take over the political institutions in Scotland, the Cardinal's response was:

'I sincerely hope not. We've surely got to work together in unity and friendship. We have to give our best talents for the good of the *whole* community, independent of race or creed, so that the Catholic Church may be a more committed Church.'

'My thoughts on that Tuesday evening of 2nd June 1982,' added Cardinal Gray, 'went back to the evening when the crowd had gathered (just close on fifty years before) at the primary school nearby in Canaan Lane.

'Christian Unity may still be far away, but the winds of change have been gently blowing. In my 34 years as a bishop I have seen the mists slowly clearing and our mutual inter-denominational and inter-Church suspicions gradually give way to an acknowledgment of sincerity in those with whose religious beliefs and theological teaching we cannot agree with nor accept. Hatred now has given way to love – "There is no fear in love," said St John (1st Epistle 4:8). "Perfect love drives out all fear".'

Ten days later, following the Pope's visit, Bishop James Monaghan, auxiliary bishop of Edinburgh and President of the Scottish Catholic Justice and Peace Commission, said in St Mary's Cathedral at the sixth hour of prayer service held by Edinburgh Churches to mark the UN special session on disarmament:

'The present war being waged between Britain and Argentina is out of all proportion to what can be achieved.'

CHAPTER 14

Closure and Retirement

FOR Cardinal Gray, even after the Papal visit, there were still times of anguish, of personal questioning and stress. Mother Teresa of Calcutta had called to see him. After a few moments of conversation, she seemed to look right into him.

'What's wrong,' she asked. 'You're worried. Will you tell me why?'

'Well,' said the Cardinal, hesitating, 'I *am* worried. We have lost four priests – since the Papal visit.'

'That is sad,' she answered, 'a heavy cross. But remember what Jesus said: "If anyone will be my disciple, let him take up his cross and follow me".'

'But it's not the kind of cross I want just now, Mother,' he replied. 'They were fine men with a great potential and we need them.'

'I don't suppose Jesus wanted the Cross,' she replied: '"Father, if it be possible, let this chalice pass from me. Yet not what I want, but what you want." Remember, He gave man free will and even God cannot force man to do what He wants. If God can't, you can't. You would have more reason to worry if you had no cross to carry.'

Prior to the Papal visit, diocesan statistics for priests and religious men and women had shown an increase from 1951, when Gordon Gray was made Archbishop. There were 20 more diocesan priests, but the number of Catholics had risen by 12,000 and that of parishes from 74 to 111. There were also new commitments – new universities and colleges, new prisons, and Bauchi, Nigeria, which covered an area as big as Scotland itself.

Since Vatican II (1962) according to the Catholic Directory, some 32 secular priests had left the priesthood in the Archdiocese of St Andrews and Edinburgh (this compared with some 41 priests leaving between 1900 and 1962). Five had left in 1969, and in the following year, the crisis-point in vocations, eleven left. Over the previous five years, the Cardinal pointed out, 13 priests had died, eight retired, seven left the priesthood and one had gone on to become a bishop!

To deal with these pressing difficulties, the Cardinal, late in 1982, put forward a comprehensive four-part plan: the sharing of resources between parishes; a reduction in the number of Sunday Masses; a greater acceptance of the participation of lay people as ministers of the Eucharist, as catechists and as home visitors; lastly, the training of permanent deacons. In addition, the Cardinal announced the setting-up of a planned approach to give Catholics a firm foundation in the Scriptures and in the teaching of the Church.

He then appealed to his priests to trust the laity and not to fear a take-over, and directed their attention to the great social problems which existed in the Archdiocese – deprived areas of Craigmillar and Pilton, of Bingham and the Raploch; the spiritual needs of Livingston and Wester Hailes; the escalating unemployment in Bathgate and Falkirk; the lack of Catholic secondary education in the Borders and East Lothian.

In the summer of the following year, Cardinal Gray revealed his alarm at the increasing number of parents who, over the past ten years, had chosen to send their children to non-denominational schools. This was particularly serious in Edinburgh, especially in view of impending rationalisation measures about to be taken by the Education authorities. He pleaded, in a letter read at all Masses in the City of Edinburgh on 19th June 1983, for parents who were thinking of sending their children to a non-denominational school, to think again: 'I ask the whole Catholic community to support their local Catholic school.'

One of the younger priests charged with the task of preparing the archdiocese for the challenges that lay ahead, was Father Michael Burns, who was episcopal vicar for pastoral spirituality. He recalls that 'Cardinal Gray played an inspirational part in the Papal visit to Scotland. His efforts at that time were centred on ensuring that the visit was a spiritual and a pastoral occasion.

'Afterwards, the Cardinal was exhausted. I remember feeding back to him comments from the organisers of the youth event. He sat in silence, then placed his hands on his head, saying, "My head is buzzing". He stood up and walked out to take his dog Rusty for a stroll!

'Later, he returned and entered into our conversation with renewed vigour. "We need all the gifts of the Holy Spirit," he said, as he looked into the challenge of the Papal visit.

'That moment was for me a watershed in our diocese. This eminent pastor had led us through the transition to Vatican II. Now he was nearing the end of his active ministry and he saw the need for a new vision, an ecclesial renewal and knew he did not have the physical strength to energise the action which was required. It was the beginning of a slow, painstaking re-assessment of our diocesan pastoral life in the light of Gospel values.'

The problem of the exodus of younger men from the priesthood, however (seen from the point of view of the former priests themselves), lay in their perception of existing clerical structures and status as being out of touch with contemporary needs. To such former priests, clerical life – as it was defined and regulated by structures established during the Counter-Reformation and specifically by the Council of Trent (1545-63) – had been re-ordered by the Second Vatican Council. Hence, between senior clergy and those priests ordained after or towards the end of the Second Vatican Council, there existed a cultural dissonance which required foresight, leadership and decisiveness to resolve constructively.

Unhappily, most senior clergy were administrators, trained in running and maintaining a well-tried system. They were generally not leaders who felt confident in breaking new ground.

Cardinal Gray was no different in this respect – he was on the whole, on the domestic front (in contrast to his great missionary initiative in Nigeria and his work internationally with the Vatican commissions or with ICEL), an administrator who at times, it seemed, found it hard to make decisions over difficult matters when they presented him with dilemmas, worry or sleepless nights.

What the young priests at the time felt they needed was proper supervision, practical and professional guidance and the means of evaluating their work. Many did not get it.

This was not a problem confined to Scotland – it was world-wide. Clericalism was in decline, but most clergy, including Cardinal Gray, did what they thought they were supposed to do and tried to stem the tide. Those young men who joined the clerical structure but wanted to be priests without it, frequently left.

Some time before the Papal visit, Cardinal Gray had written to the Pope, requesting that he be permitted to retire from his episcopal responsibilities. He felt he had made out a solid case. He was then in his 73rd year and had served as Archbishop for over 31 years.

His health had deteriorated, especially the spinal trouble brought on by digging, carrying heavy loads, laying three-by-two cement slabs. The result was to be seen during the visit of Pope John Paul to Ireland, when the Cardinal had slipped three discs.

He approached the Pope in November of 1983 when, after the Papal visit to Scotland, the members of the Scottish Bishops' Conference travelled to Rome to make their quinquennial *Ad Limina* progress report.

He explained in person to the Pope that he had slowed down, physically and mentally, and was no longer personally mobile. He had also, after 50 years of driving, lost his confidence in handling a car. He spoke to John Paul about his failing memory, of his fear of making decisions that might eventually embarrass his successor. The Pope listened patiently, but asked him to remain in office until he reached the age of 75.

Gordon Joseph also had a long talk with Cardinal Sebastiano Baggio, then Prefect for the Congregation of Bishops. He was charming, told him he fully understood his problems (being not far short of his age), and asked him to carry on until he was 75.

Cardinal Gray went home with mixed feelings. Happy in one sense, for retirement was an unknown quantity; unhappy, because he knew he was less capable of facing big decisions and was unable to satisfy himself that the diocese was not suffering from his physical and intellectual weaknesses.

So he carried on, knowing that a younger, more active, more daring, more forward-looking man was required. In the autumn of 1984 he wrote again, pleading to be allowed to retire.

Archbishop Heim, the Apostolic Nuncio, discussed the situation with him and agreed to recommend that his request be granted. In January 1985 he received word that the Holy Father had acquiesced, but that official retirement would be delayed until the announcement of his successor.

Of course, the mass media were anticipating his retirement when he was 75, and there were bound to be information leaks. So in February the Cardinal decided to jump the gun and, in a letter to his clergy, announced that the Pope had accepted his resignation and that his successor's name would be announced in due course. That left the speculators free to speculate and he had a little more peace than he would otherwise have enjoyed.

But there were still serious problems for the Cardinal to cope with. In 1985, for example, a campaign of vilification came to a head when the president of a Roman decastery, The Pontifical Council for the Family, wrote to the Apostolic Delegate, Archbishop Bruno Heim, complaining of the apostolate of Father Andrew Monaghan (in the words of Cardinal Gray 'a good and orthodox priest'), who was engaged in counselling on a local radio programme phone-in – 'The Open Line' on Radio Forth.

He wrote because of complaints from a small number of lay persons concerning the advice this priest was accused of giving to, among a wide spectrum of problems, persons faced with sexual problems such as AIDS and abortion.

The evidence against him was a scarcely decipherable off-air tape recording of advice he had given to a distraught person who was contemplating suicide. In addition, the group of critics distributed transcripts of tapes widely across the diocese.

'I happened to have heard the broadcast,' recalled the Cardinal. 'I met with the priest in question, discussed the situation and wrote to our Apostolic Delegate, Archbishop Heim, expressing my indignation that the President of the particular Commission had reported the complaint to him, instead of myself – the Bishop of the diocese and a Cardinal.

'The Delegate was apologetic. I wrote to the Cardinal Prefect, my old friend Cardinal James R Knox, and enclosed a long and carefully-prepared dossier on the case, and a description of the circumstances that, in our country, legally required non-directive counselling. He agreed with the information submitted and the case was closed.'

However, on the death of Cardinal Knox, a new Prefect, Cardinal Edouard Gagnon, was appointed. The case was raised once more by the new President.

'He who has never heard the programme,' the Cardinal continued, 'but has read complaints from persons whom we know to be misinformed and opposed to the priest – demands that this thoroughly orthodox priest should be silenced.

'My successor, Archbishop O'Brien, has written long memoranda,' pointed out the Cardinal, 'supported by our present Pro-Nuncio and myself. But still, this Prefect demands that this thoroughly orthodox priest should be taken off the programme. My successor is still insisting on his rights, as Archbishop, to make his own decisions and not to be interfered with by a Roman official who has no knowledge of the local circumstances.'

Officially, Gordon Joseph Gray retired as Archbishop of St Andrews and Edinburgh on 30th May 1985, when his successor, Father Keith O'Brien, was publicly nominated to the See.

The Cardinal fulfilled his programme of engagements until the new Archbishop's ordination on 5th August 1985. He then gradually withdrew from public life.

'I am glad that I was able to be the principal ordaining bishop for Keith Patrick's ordination,' commented the Cardinal later. 'It was touch-and-go, for my back was bad that day – agonising. But I got through and it was a wonderful occasion.'

The bishops, clergy and the Archbishop were anxious that he should continue to stay at St Bennet's, where he had been resident for 34 years. But he had always been deeply conscious of financial resources and had sacrificed much to keep the diocese from getting into the red so that there might be some reserve capital for emergencies. He had even put some of his family legacies into this fund.

Moreover, the garden was growing bigger as he grew older! St Margaret's Convent, where his mother, two sisters and two nieces had been educated, had a house in the grounds that was used for visitors. It was in a state of disrepair. However, the Ursuline Sisters said he might have it. And so he moved in beside what was the first post-Reformation religious house in Scotland, close to the Gothic pinnacles of Gillespie Graham's Chapel of 1835, where he was able to celebrate Mass and join in the prayer-life of the Gillis College seminarians. As age and illness slowly overcame him, he was able also to preside from his wheelchair at the many community services where the Chapel would be crowded with young people.

The Cardinal also presided from his wheelchair in St Mary's Cathedral, Broughton Street, at all the major events that occurred there.

Perhaps the last and greatest event was when he again welcomed Mother Teresa to the Cathedral just a few weeks before his death. He continued to give a fine example to all the priests of the diocese in that he celebrated the Chrism Mass each year during Holy Week. There, he pledged his commitment to priestly service. And he rejoiced at travelling throughout the diocese to celebrate the jubilees of priests and religious.

Although the Hermitage, built around 1856 in the Scottish Baronial style, was rather small, he never wanted to live in better quarters, nor with a greater income than his fellow priests in retirement. The Cardinal carried out major repairs to his new home and a little modernisation. Using a generous gift on the occasion of his retirement given to him by the diocesan clergy, he renovated the house and moved in accompanied by his Cairn terrier, Rusty, and the Sister who served him at St Bennet's for 15 years, Sister Cyril Griffin. Behind him he left his library, his gardening tools and his workshop – all of which he missed greatly.

When the Cardinal moved in, the house was in a state of chaos. The Cardinal decided to give himself a sabbatical year to acclimatise to his new surroundings. He took up residence on the 1st of October 1985, whilst the workmen were still completing the job under the guidance of his great friend of more than 25 years, the retired Clerk of Works, Robert Murray, an elder in his Kirk. He was not only a Clerk of Works, but a skilled and qualified joiner, a cabinet-maker, and a man of many practical skills.

During the final years of his retirement, various events made necessary by the retrenchment of the Church in Scotland during a period of contraction, saddened the Cardinal deeply.

He was particularly affected by the merger (1981) and closure (1984) of the former Craiglockhart College of Education, and the subsequent closures of the junior seminary of Blairs and the senior seminary of Drygrange in June 1986. Although the former was replaced by a vocations scheme, and the latter transferred to the complex at Gillis College in Edinburgh, nevertheless the Cardinal, although free from direct administrative responsibility, felt some measure of their failure should be attributed to him as the senior clerical figure in the Scottish Church.

A true Scot at heart, faced with the loss of these institutions which he had carefully nurtured over the years, he warned, 'We must appreciate the importance of our roots. I am Scottish to the marrow of my bones. I want Scotland to be one, and not only politically'.

Commenting on the 3rd of July on the Campaign for a Scottish Assembly, the Cardinal revealed that 'being a good Scotsman, I am naturally keen to see some form of devolution in order to secure betterment for our country. I have sympathies with this movement, but I am not at all interested in separatism.'

In retirement, Cardinal Gray used his unique position to fight for Scotland's right to have its own independent life and industry. In a letter published in a number of newspapers on 18th May 1990, he deplored the decision to close the Ravenscraig steel mill:

'The passing of the years has done nothing to dim my pride and my Scottish identity and my love for all that is best in our national life. Much more than steel was forged in the work place of one of our great and traditional industries.

'A good deal of the Scottish character was shaped there too – camaraderie, friendship, clear-sightedness about goals and accomplishments. Many of our traditional industries have gone. Where they have been replaced by new jobs and a better way of life, I have no complaint.

'All too often what has come in their place is at the mercy of a control which is not in Scottish hands. Many of them are beyond the influence of a non-interventionist Government, a Government which places a singular reliance on market forces. But there is no morality in market forces. Their value lies in the coldness of their economic logic. This is abundantly clear in the recent decision of British Steel to kill the Scottish steel industry.'

In August 1990 he reached his 80th birthday and, according to Vatican regulations introduced by Pope John Paul II, he retired from active duty with the College of Cardinals in Rome.

He continued to practise his religion, not as an external habit, but as an internal conviction – in his own words: 'Some folk's religion is like a wooden leg – no life or warmth in it. They strap it on each morning. It certainly helps them to hobble along, but it never is part of themselves.'

At this time he re-emphasised that he had great confidence in the future of Christianity and of Scotland being in the hands of young people: 'They are a praying and caring group and the evidence of this is shown in their interest in justice and peace issues.

'The most important thing I feel I have done in my life,' he added, 'is being a shepherd to my people. The most significant thing I have seen is the coming together of the various Christian Churches in the Ecumenical movement.'

On 24th December 1990, Cardinal Gray was taken to Edinburgh Royal Infirmary, having suffered another severe heart-attack and cardiac arrest, but was resuscitated after seven or eight minutes. Subsequently, he was kept in the coronary care unit until he was discharged on 16th January 1991.

In the course of 1991, Bell's Palsy developed, following a worsening of his arthritic condition and a baker's cyst behind his knee. His general mobility deteriorated, but he continued to attend public services, presiding from his wheelchair.

Late in 1992 came another heavy blow. The impending closure of Gillis College, the only senior seminary in the East of Scotland, was announced – it was, to the Cardinal, like turning a knife in a deep wound. The Scottish Bishops took the decision to amalgamate the college at Gillis with Chesters College in Glasgow. Imitating the widespread rationalisation of resources in many other fields, a new Scottish national seminary would be created later in 1993, the realisation of a very old dream.

Following a formal Declaration from Rome of the acknowledgment of the Scottish theologian and Franciscan monk, John Duns Scotus as *Blessed*, the Cardinal wrote to his successor, Archbishop Keith Patrick O'Brien:

'I realise that a national seminary has been an objective for close on a century. The sooner the two colleges (Gillis and Chesters) die, the sooner the united national college can be baptised into new life with a new name.

'My suggestion, perhaps obvious, is that the national seminary be called Scotus College. Now that John Duns Scotus is recognised as a theologian by the Church of Scotland, as well as by ourselves, he could indeed be the road to unity – especially now with the existence of Action of Churches Together in Scotland (ACTS).'

Cardinal Gray felt he could see (in the phrase of the Second Vatican Council) an *aggiornamento* – a bringing up-to-date. In the same letter, the Cardinal added, 'Our sacrifice of Gillis might well be the opening of a new door to Christian unity in our country. I feel happier now in my conviction that the closing of Gillis College may well be the price we must pay, that "They may be one, as thou, Father, in me and I in you, that they may be one in us". I can now pray for the national college with peace in my heart – which I had not, before the surprise news about John Duns Scotus.' Happily, his suggestion was gladly accepted by the Scottish Bishops.

Increasingly, Cardinal Gray was being overcome by a painful combination of past and present illness – Bell's Palsy, arthritis, a stroke and partial blindness. He faced the closeness of death with courage:

'To anticipate is the great adventure of death. Then, we shall see what eyes cannot yet contemplate,' he had written on a piece of paper inserted behind a photograph of his parents – and some verses:

> *I walked down the valley of silence,*
> *Down the deep silent valley alone,*
> *And heard the sound of no footsteps*
> *Around me, save God's and my own.*

There were still many grounds for him to be joyful – the care and concern of countless friends and admirers, and the peaceful cultivation of his garden which brought him so much contentment, both physical and spiritual.

'In my former home at St Bennet's we were able to display a dazzling array of flowers (including at least 700 roses) and feed ourselves from the vegetables we grew. An hour or so very early in the morning was a good time for digging and planting.

'Now I am retired, I still have a little garden. The good Sister who looks after my house is a farmer's daughter, loves the land and has green fingers.

'In the garden she does most of the heavier work. But I can still relax in God's lovely creation and plant the seeds, prick them out and pot them up.

'Before the liturgical revival, one of the most popular prayer books was *The Garden of the Soul*. The garden each spring comes to new life, to a resurrection. Our Lord's Easter greeting was "Peace be with you".

'I always liked *The Garden of the Soul* and in my garden I share the Peace of the Risen Christ. We rarely purchase packets of seeds these days. We gather them when the flowers fade. We dry them and plant them in the spring. And as they germinate, we feel that we are preparing to display for Jesus, the Divine and Creative Gardener, a little and beautiful corner of the new Eden, the Paradise we hope eternally to enjoy.

'When my time comes, despite my failings, I hope He may give me a little patch in the heavenly garden to dig and weed, to plant and give pleasure to all the dear souls who had to live in the high-rise flats during their days on earth.'

Cardinal Gray's last public Mass was concelebrated with his successor, Archbishop O'Brien, and some of the priests of the diocese, in Gillis College Chapel at half past seven on the morning of Tuesday 6th July 1993 – just two weeks before his death.

The Mass was to mark the beginning of the Archdiocesan Pilgrimage to the shrine of the Virgin Mary at Lourdes. After the Mass, the Cardinal, sitting in his wheelchair, led the procession of pilgrims to his beloved grotto in the grounds of the College, its statue of the Virgin surrounded by flowers. Then he turned and spoke to the pilgrims in the sunshine: 'I envy you your pilgrim-age to Lourdes. Pray for me, as Sister Cyril and I will pray for you each day at this shrine during your absence.'

Unhappily, the Cardinal was not able to keep that promise. On 14th July he was re-admitted to the Royal Infirmary. His heart was failing and he was fitted with a pacemaker. Just as the Lourdes Pilgrimage was drawing to a close, so too his own life on earth was coming to an end.

Among the many friends who visited him was Father Leo Glancy, parish priest of St Catherine's, Gracemount, who had for a number of years conducted an apostolate for the sick and the deaf, and was also one of the Cardinal's *Fidei Donum* priests in Nigeria, and, for five years, spiritual director at Gillis College.

'I asked him if he would like to receive the Sacrament of the Sick,' said Father Glancy later. 'The Cardinal nodded eagerly and with quiet faith. I anointed the powerful hands which had once rested on my head in ordination 30 years ago. I listened for the last time to his rich voice saying the prayers.'

Some time later, Father Glancy heard that the Cardinal's con-dition was beyond the help of a pacemaker. He then telephoned Archbishop O'Brien to say that he would be happy to stay with the Cardinal on the Sunday night.

It was just after midnight when Sister Cyril said goodnight and the Cardinal mumbled a response. Father Glancy sat down beside the bed.

'I began my vigil with the Prayer of the Church and continued with the Rosary. The night passed quickly. The Cardinal was a little restless at times. His right hand would slip down by the bedside. As I held his hand and prayed the Rosary, touching his fingers, he was very peaceful. It seemed to me that I was repre-senting the praying Church, all those on whom, over the past years, the Cardinal had laid his hands in conferring Sacraments.

'We need one another in the Body of Christ. When one member is weak, knowing of the support of those to whom we belong is comforting – like a child who clings to its mother.

'Sometime after, the hand which, in prayer, had clutched at the Body of Christ, opened – ready to receive all that the Lord had to offer. A symbol of the prayer of abandonment to God's own love.'

At six in the morning on Monday 19th July 1993 the Cardinal's housekeeper, Sister Cyril, arrived to say the morning prayer. Father Glancy went over to visit another patient, before returning home to bed.

At the bedside in the hospital, where he rested for the last morning of his earthly life, was Archbishop O'Brien, auxiliary bishop Bishop Kevin Rafferty, along with the vicars general Monsignor Patrick Grady and Monsignor Anthony McNally, and Father Anthony Duffy, the diocesan treasurer.

Representatives of the Cardinal's family were also present, as well as Sister Cyril, the Cardinal's dedicated housekeeper for over 20 years. The prayers for the dying were softly recited and, as the end was nearing, Sister Cyril placed a lighted candle in the Cardinal's hands.

Slowly, he breathed his last. Then Sister Cyril quietly extinguished the light of the candle.

*　　*　　*

Over the days that followed, thousands of people from all over Scotland gathered in prayer at Gillis College and then at St Mary's Cathedral to pray before the body of the Cardinal as it lay in state.

Wonderful tributes were paid to the Cardinal from all sectors of the population through the medium of television, radio and the press. An avalanche of mail arrived at Archbishop's House.

Ending his homily during the Funeral Mass, Archbishop O'Brien, the Cardinal's successor, referred to the words which the Cardinal had used when preaching in the Cathedral in his retirement, on the occasion of the 175th anniversary of its foundation (15th August 1989):

'I have seen and admired great medieval and modern cathedrals and the basilicas of many lands. Yet for me, St Mary's Cathedral is the most beloved Gate of Heaven and House of God, through which and in which, I hope one day to enter into life.'

At the end of Mass, the Cardinal's remains were lowered carefully and simply into the Cathedral crypt. Two sprays of flowers were placed on the coffin – one from his family, the other from Sister Cyril and her own sister, Sister Hyacinth.

In that Cathedral, which he had loved so much and from whose pulpit he had fearlessly proclaimed the Word of God, 'in season and out of season', Cardinal Gordon Joseph Gray now rests, awaiting the Resurrection and that entry into new life for which he had so often longed.

APPENDIX

Posthumous Tributes

The Revd Douglas AITKEN
~ CHURCH OF SCOTLAND ~

For nearly two decades I worked in the religious broad-
casting department of the BBC and got to know, love and
respect Cardinal Gray as a fine, gracious and deeply committed man. On the many occasions we met, he never
regarded me as one of a different denomination; he saw me
as a fellow Christian and always reached for those things we
had in common. I hope that, in his eyes, I did the same.

19th September 1993

The Very Revd Professor Robin S BARBOUR
~ Former Moderator of the GENERAL ASSEMBLY
of the CHURCH OF SCOTLAND 1979 ~

There must be a huge number of people like me, not members of the same Church but followers of Christ, who found
in Gordon Gray a real colleague and fellow worker. He
certainly did an enormous amount to dispel the ugly shad-
ows of past mistrust and prejudice: a wonderful servant of
his Lord and ours.

One of my most vivid memories of him is of the great
service and Mass in Aberdeen when Bishop Mario Conti was
installed (3rd May 1977). I don't think I am likely ever to
forget his features as he celebrated Mass – here was a man

for whom worship, and the Sacrament in particular, were
the very heart of everything that life is about. His rugged
face was transfigured – that is the only word.

31st August 1993

The Revd Maxwell CRAIG
~ ACTION OF CHURCHES TOGETHER IN SCOTLAND (ACTS) ~

We, in Action of Churches Together in Scotland, give thanks
to God for Gordon's leadership, for his faithfulness and for
his commitment to the unity of Scottish Christians.

I personally treasure his part in the dedication of St
Columba's parish church, Bridge of Don, where I was privileged to serve as minister before coming to Dunblane.

21st July 1993

The Very Revd Professor Robert CRAIG
~ Former Moderator of the GENERAL ASSEMBLY
of the CHURCH OF SCOTLAND 1986 ~

My first meeting with Gordon Gray was in October 1935
when we both matriculated at St Andrews University as
students in the Faculty of Arts. During the following three
years, we sat together in Latin, Natural Science, History,
Philosophy and English classes. He was well read in medieval and spoken Latin, but, so far as I remember, his
classical Latin was not much better than mine.

He distinguished himself in Philosophy and in English,
and went on in his fourth year to take an Honours degree in
English. During these four years he combined the two full-
time occupations of student and assistant to his uncle, Canon
Gray, at St James' Church on the Scores.

Thereafter, our paths separated, but we kept in touch by
letter and by my visits to see him during my leaves from
abroad.

In 1967 he and I were on the same platform to receive the honorary DD of St Andrews. He was the first Roman Catholic since the Reformation to be so honoured.

During my Moderatorial year (1986-87), I frequently visited Cardinal Gray in Edinburgh at his retirement home, the Hermitage. It was then that I came to appreciate his life and work more fully.

The abysmal and deplorable state of Protestant–Catholic relations in Scotland fifty years ago was such that, even at local level, parish minister and parish priest were commonly hardly on speaking terms, and there was little communication at higher levels.

In the intervening half century it became possible for Protestants to recognise that the Reformation was not entirely an unmixed blessing, and for Roman Catholics to see in the Reformation the recovery of certain lost truths in the Christian faith.

To have maintained, as he did, the essentials of his own Roman Catholic position, while extending charity, humanity, goodwill and tolerance to us who differed from him, was the test of both his integrity and his diplomacy.

In this, Cardinal Gray so succeeded that the transformation of Protestant–Roman Catholic relations in our time in Scotland must be seen, humanly speaking, as largely his work.

25th September 1993

Cardinal Cahal DALY,
Archbishop of Armagh
~ CATHOLIC CHURCH ~

An Edinburgh man by birth and by a lifetime of pastoral care, as priest, Archbishop and Cardinal, he spent himself untiringly in the work of the Kingdom of God and the upbuilding of the Church in his native archdiocese, which he passionately loved and devotedly served.

A true Scotsman, he was greatly respected by his countrymen from all religious backgrounds and from all walks of life.

He valued the close historic links between Scotland and Ireland and between his own archdiocese and the Church in Ireland. He had many Irish friends and visited Ireland on many occasions.

In the beautiful words of an Irish prayer:

> O King who are kindly and without gloom,
> in the city of Graces,
> carry him up with you
> high above the sound of the waters
> giving praise for evermore
> to the Lamb who was put to death for us.

19th July 1993

Episcopal Bishop Michael Hare DUKE
~ SCOTTISH EPISCOPAL CHURCH ~

I came to Scotland as the Bishop of St Andrews in 1969, but in the five years before Vatican II, I remember very little contact with the Scottish Catholic hierarchy.

There was one eccumenical service in St Mungo's Cathedral, Glasgow, the Church of Scotland High Kirk, where, because Archbishop Scanlan was present, the lunatic fringe of the Reformed churches demonstrated wildly. But then the climate changed. Perhaps because relations were easier with the Bishops of the Episcopal Church, there no longer seemed to be the barrier that opponents of ecumenism could seek to exploit.

Under Cardinal Gray's chairmanship, the two sets of bishops began to meet regularly for study. In St Andrews, Cardinal Gray preached from John Knox's pulpit in the University church of St Salvator's. On occasions of historical significance he, as Bishop of St Andrews and Edinburgh, and I, as Bishop of St Andrews, Dunkeld and Dunblane, were able to share in acts of worship with little cause for comment.

As well as breaking new ground ecumenically, which stemmed directly from Vatican II, Cardinal Gray's thinking in social affairs bore marks of the *perestroika* which had opened the thinking of Rome. The new departures were not undertaken grudgingly or tentatively, but boldly and with a due acknowledgment of the risks involved.

In particular, when the Catholic Bishops' Conference of America was in process of preparing their revolutionary pastoral letter on nuclear weapons, Father Frank Winter SJ was researching the statements of the Catholic Conferences of Europe. The statement by the Scottish hierarchy was by far the most outspoken against nuclear weapons of any European Conference of Catholic Bishops.

In these as in other ways, it was clear that Gordon Gray was sufficiently confident in his faith to take the risks of new thinking and new action. While the unsure hedge their bets and make tentative advances, those who have a confident faith in God, step forward boldly and risk much in the service of the generous and sustaining master whom they know.

6th October 1993

Episcopal Bishop Alastair HAGGART
~ SCOTTISH EPISCOPAL CHURCH ~

One of the first things Gordon and I started was the Roman Catholic and Episcopal bishops meeting once a quarter regularly.

We discussed all kinds of things which affected the Christian good of Scotland education, social affairs and the National movement.

I also saw him after he retired at the Hermitage in Whitehouse Loan. He was essentially a guardian, a conserver rather than a prophet, a conservative with a small c.

He was a very liberal-hearted man, but shrewd in his social and political judgments. He was a man who had a tremendously powerful ecclesiastical as well as ecclesial sense, but who believed that the ecclesial had to be contained by the ecclesiastical. He admitted that defects and errors existed in the ecclesiastical structure, but emphasised the ecclesial integrity of the Church, like John Paul II's phrase – 'the kernel of the nut'. He would concede all kinds of things about the nut, but was very protective of the kernel.

I once asked him – 'You were a bishop at 40 and have been one for almost 40 years. You've lived through a most astonishing revolution?'

'When I became Archbishop of St Andrews and Edinburgh,' replied the Cardinal, 'I could look around the diocese and see things which needed to be done. I could identify and consult those people I believed competent or trustworthy. I made decisions and appointed people. Now, I can't blow my nose without setting up a commission to advise me! A lot of time is wasted in setting up such bodies.'

In the early years of his episcopate Gordon believed he knew the people best qualified to do a particular job. Whoever he appointed was answerable to him. Today, all kinds of people were appointed who were better at talking than acting, and bishops were under pressure to follow decisions of advisory bodies they had little say in appointing.

In his heart he was much more committed to ecumenism than in his mind or will. There was often a tension between heart and what he knew was the official position of the Church, but his will was totally committed to the Church. Those who were not Roman Catholics sometimes found difficulty in reconciling his personal warmth and openness with his hard-line, conservative decision-making.

His great achievement was that he shifted the way in which the generality of people in Scotland regarded the Roman Catholic Church, just as Cardinal Hume has done in England, but each did so in a very different manner.

Cardinal Gray projected the image of an ordinary, down-to-earth man from the Borders – his family origins in Banff and his birth in Leith were historical accidents – and these qualities helped smooth the course of the Papal visit to Scotland in 1982. He was the kind of man whose generosity of heart commended the Roman Catholic Church to many. He was a good man to know.

14th September 1993

The Revd John HARVEY
~ Leader of the IONA COMMUNITY ~

When I was a parish minister in Stirling in the seventies, I had occasion to correspond with Cardinal Gray in connection with the health of my colleague there, the parish priest. Both Cardinal Gray and I were trying to persuade him to move to a quiet and less demanding post: but I'm afraid our combined efforts were in vain! However, I was much struck with the humanity, love and friendliness of the Cardinal: qualities which clearly have impressed all who knew him.

21st July 1993

The Very Revd Andrew HERRON
~ Former Moderator of the GENERAL ASSEMBLY
of the CHURCH OF SCOTLAND 1971 ~

I had an enormous respect and regard for Cardinal Gray, but my actual connections with him were all of the trivial and superficial kind. Were I to try to put something of our occasional encounters into words, I should say, 'We spoke the same language'.

30th August 1993

The Revd Alan P HORNER
~ METHODIST CHURCH IN SCOTLAND ~

When I came to Scotland as Chairman of the Methodist Synod in 1982, Cardinal Gray was already a household name, and greatly respected by Christians of other traditions, including my own. I soon found out why, and came to value his contribution to any gathering or discussion.

We met from time to time in the context of gatherings of Church Leaders in Edinburgh in which the personal contact was as important as the agenda. Methodism is numerically small in Scotland, but Gordon Gray always affirmed us and made us feel included and wanted. Although a busy man, with many things to occupy him, he remembered names and welcomed ideas, respecting each contribution whether or not he could agree with it.

My most vivid memory of him is of the occasion at Scottish Churches House, Dunblane, when he introduced the Papal Nuncio, and we received as a gift the spinning wheel which had been presented to the Pope on his visit to Scotland in 1982. The gift and the photograph are on display in the Conference Room, and represent for me a visible and tangible link with the Pope's visit which took place before I came to Scotland; and with the Cardinal whom I was privileged to meet and know.

Such links were an essential prelude to the growing relationship, deepening trust, and warmth of friendship which are increasingly an accepted part of inter-Church life in Scotland today.

20th November 1993

Cardinal Basil HUME,
Archbishop of Westminster
~ CATHOLIC CHURCH ~

Cardinal Gordon Gray gave generous and unstinting service as both priest and bishop to the Catholic community in Scotland and the wider Church over many years.

He pioneered many initiatives in the Church's ecumenical endeavour and made a particular contribution to the Church's growing appreciation of mass communications.

He also played a leading role in guiding the changes from Latin to English in the Church's worship.

In all his activities he was first and foremost a priest and at heart always a concerned shepherd of his people.

His was a long and fruitful Episcopal ministry.

23rd July 1993

The Rt Hon Norman IRONS
~ LORD PROVOST OF EDINBURGH ~

I knew Cardinal Gray personally over a period of many years and I know that he will be greatly missed – not only because he was highly respected, but because of the immense warmth and friendliness of his personality.

He was a significant figure in religious activities in Edinburgh and Scotland over many decades. Christians of all denominations in our country recognised, and continue to benefit from, his constructive work in building ecumenical relations. His stature as a churchman was as great as his physical presence and I know that people of all religious denominations and of none were sorry to learn of his death.

3rd August 1993

Pope JOHN PAUL II
~ CATHOLIC CHURCH ~

I have learnt with sadness of the death of Cardinal Gordon Joseph Gray and offer heartfelt condolences to the Archdiocese of St Andrews and Edinburgh and to the whole Church in Scotland.

Grateful for the Cardinal's many years of distinguished service to the Church, and mindful of his outstanding example of humble dedication, I invoke upon him eternal rest in the peace of Christ and impart my apostolic blessing to all who mourn him in the sure hope of the Resurrection.

23rd July 1993

The Very Revd William B JOHNSTON
~ Former Moderator of the GENERAL ASSEMBLY
of the CHURCH OF SCOTLAND 1980 ~

My first meeting with Gordon Gray was at a conference at Drygrange. These were the days just after Vatican II, when contacts between the Church of Scotland and the Roman Catholic Church were regular and frequent, and when a group of theologians from both Churches met regularly at Drygrange to discuss theological topics under Monsignor John Barry and the late Dr Rudolph Ehrlich.

To one of these came the new Archbishop – young, friendly and huggable – anxious to hear what we in the Kirk had to say on a wide range of issues.

He was, I remember, very attentive to the paper that I was due to read on a New Testament subject, and he asked many relevant questions, both during the discussion and over tea afterwards. This was the beginning of a friendship that lasted until his death.

Our friendship grew much closer in the arrangements for the visit of the Pope in 1982. It so happened that when I was Moderator in 1980-81, the decision was made that the Pope would visit the UK in 1982. Gordon Gray (by then Cardinal) sent me a letter to inform me ahead of the press releases, so that the Church of Scotland was kept in the picture.

On the day that Gordon Gray retired it was, by chance, my turn to do the 'Thought for the Day' on BBC Radio Scotland, so I mentioned this happening to Gordon and received from him a typically courteous letter of thanks.

Our last meeting was through an intermediary. We were both in separate hospitals and an official of the Health Board visited me. The official had just been to see Gordon who had bidden him to bring me a message of greetings to the effect that, since we were both in the same boat, he would be glad if we could pray for each other. That was typical, for at bottom he was also a man of deep spiritual power for whom prayer was a way of life. I cherished his friendship while he was alive, as I cherish his memory now that he has gone.

30th September 1993

The Right Revd L E LUSCOMBE
~ Formerly Primus of the SCOTTISH EPISCOPAL CHURCH ~

My first contact with Cardinal Gray was during a joint
meeting of the Scottish hierarchy and the Bishops of the
Episcopal Church. These twice-yearly events began during
his cardinalate. I remember that I came away with a new
appreciation of the word 'eminence' which was, of course,
part of his official title. Gordon Gray's eminence had a depth
and breadth to it over and above the normal connotation of
height. He would not have been out of place cast in the role
of one of those two angelic messengers at the scene of the
Lord's ascension who brought the disciples back to reality
and to a sense of mission.

Both as a young bishop and after my election as Primus,
he treated me with the utmost courtesy and friendliness. I
recall in particular one afternoon when we spoke at length
of the common problems affecting our seminaries; he with
Gillis College so obviously dear to his heart, and me with
Coates Hall in the West End of Edinburgh. With the wisdom
of hindsight, I wish now that we had pursued some of the
ideas that we shared that day.

There is a phrase in the canticle *Benedicite Omnia Opera* –
'O all ye holy and humble men of heart'. Of such was, and
is, Gordon Gray.

24th November 1993

The Very Revd Professor John McINTYRE
~ Former Moderator of the GENERAL ASSEMBLY
of the CHURCH OF SCOTLAND 1982 ~

It was not my good fortune to have been a long-standing
friend of the Cardinal, as were some of my colleagues. It was
during the visit of Pope John Paul II that I came to know
him. This event, in so many ways the climax of the Cardinal's
career, fell within the year in which I was Moderator of the

General Assembly of the Church of Scotland. Several things impressed me about the way in which the Cardinal arranged things.

For example, at a very early stage in the planning of the details of the visit, he made it plain that an opportunity should be given to the Church of Scotland to make its own expression of welcome and goodwill towards the Holy Father. The visit was an occasion of joyous celebration for the Roman Catholic Church, understandably so – yet he was magnanimous enough to invite us to share in the great occasion. It is very difficult to measure the quality and the dimension of the contribution to ecumenical co-operation and understanding which that action achieved; but I do believe that it will prove to be of resounding historical importance.

Further, the occasions for meeting which the Cardinal facilitated were by no means perfunctory or meagre. On the evening of his arrival in Scotland, the Pope spent time meeting the past Moderators of the Church in the context of the Assembly Hall, in New College quadrangle; but more significantly – beneath the shadow of the statue of John Knox. One of the newspapers next morning printed a photograph, taken from the side, of the Pope, the statue of John Knox and myself in a line, with the caption, 'Here is the photo that took four hundred years to take!'

The Cardinal also arranged a private audience with the Pope for myself at his residence, at which we exchanged gifts, the Pope giving me a piece of silver statuary portraying the Good Shepherd with a sheep and a lamb, and myself giving him a silver quaich from the Church of Scotland.

Also, when the time came for me, as Moderator, to visit the Church of Scotland Church in Rome, the Cardinal graciously wrote letters of commendation to the Vatican, so that Mrs McIntyre and I were received in audience by the Holy Father. He had the happiest of memories of his visit to Scotland, as you can well imagine, as had we; and it was a delight and an honour to share them.

So, if it is the case that, in the parishes of Scotland, ordinary folks of different denominations have never in modern times been on better terms with one another, and are already beginning to be genuine sharers of the faith, credit must go to the quiet and gracious ecumenical dedication of the Cardinal. In a way, he saw all Scotland as his parish and we were all the better for that.

22nd September 1993

Bashir MANN
~ THE MUSLIM COMMUNITY ~

As a Glasgow baillie I used to meet Cardinal Gray annually at the Kirking of the Council. I particularly remember his way of making people – whoever he met – feel at ease.

His efforts to bring harmony to Scotland's multi-racial and multicultural society won him respect throughout the country.

He tried to break down the barriers between the different communities and denominations. These are the things I admired him for.

19th March 1993

The Revd Andrew MORTON
~ CHURCH OF SCOTLAND ~

The Board of World Mission and Unity of the Church of Scotland associates itself with the many representative Christian individuals and bodies within Scotland and beyond it that give thanks to God for the life and witness of the late Cardinal Gordon Gray.

This Board, the body responsible to our General Assembly for promoting Christian unity, is particularly conscious of the great contribution made by Cardinal Gray to the warmth and the depth of ecumenical relations which we now enjoy in this land.

21st July 1993

The Most Revd Keith O'BRIEN,
Archbishop of St Andrews and Edinburgh
~ CATHOLIC CHURCH ~

During his last illness, a taxi-driver said to one of my
brother Bishops: 'How is the Cardinal keeping now? You
know, there are three things which we like about him – his
pipe, his gardening and his dog!'

Cardinal Gray came across to the ordinary person, (as to
the person of rank), as quite simply a good, an ordinary man.

I knew the Cardinal from my own time as a schoolboy,
asking to be accepted as a student for seminary. He also
ordained me as a priest, gave me all my priestly appointments
and then ordained me as a Bishop, his successor as Archbishop of St Andrews and Edinburgh.

But, as with that taxi-driver, so also with myself and so
many others who knew him – it was Gordon Gray the man,
who held an attraction for us.

Shortly after my appointment as Archbishop and before
my ordination by the Cardinal himself, he sent a little
prayer-card to my home. On one side was printed the sen-
tence: 'Lord, help me to remember that nothing is going to
happen to me today that you and I together can't handle'.
On the reverse, the Cardinal had written: 'Hoping that this
will light up the skies when the clouds are heavy'.

Another fond memory I have of that loving, caring man
was on my return from hospital when I was suffering from
glandular fever.

I was brought back to my home in rather a weak state –
and there was the Cardinal in his wheelchair waiting to
greet me in my sitting-room.

He realised that I would want to celebrate Mass, but was
perhaps too weak to say Mass on my own.

He was the principal celebrant while I celebrated Mass at
his side. United in our love of the Lord and in the high
regard which we had for each other, he seemed to impart by
his very presence something of his own failing strength to
me.

Since his death, I have been the recipient of many letters of condolence and many tributes, paid not only by dignitaries, but by countless thousands of ordinary people.

Cardinal Gray left all the people of Scotland a precious heritage – an awareness of the importance of the individual in the sight of Almighty God.

19th March 1994

Dr N A OPPENHEIM
~ EDINBURGH HEBREW CONGREGATION ~

Although the Hebrew Congregation is aware that the late Rabbi Dr Weinberg and Cardinal Gray were friendly, and that each respected and admired the other, I am unable to ascertain from any of our sources how exactly they met, or on what basis the friendship was founded.

I know, of my own personal knowledge, of the Rabbi's appreciation of Cardinal Gray and I heard him speak, in my presence, most warmly of him, both as a man and as a religious leader. I also know that the Cardinal was instrumental in introducing the Rabbi to the Pope on his visit here.

31st October 1993

The Most Revd Daniel PILARCZYK,
Archbishop of Cincinnati
~ CATHOLIC CHURCH ~

Cardinal Gray contributed much to the establishment of the International Commission on English in the Liturgy and to the early years of its service to the Church in the English-speaking world. He was present at the first meeting of ICEL on October 17th 1963 in Rome, and he continued as a member of the Episcopal Board until his retirement from ICEL in November 1978, at which time he hosted the ICEL meetings in Edinburgh, his beloved native city.

We recall with particular gratitude Cardinal Gray's service as chairman of the Episcopal Board from 1965 to 1972. Those were busy days for ICEL, and Cardinal Gray laboured tirelessly to ensure a solid foundation for ICEL's difficult and pioneering task and to foster harmony and acceptance among the eleven member conferences of ICEL, spread literally the world over.

May the Divine Master welcome Cardinal Gray into paradise, there to receive the reward promised to the good and faithful steward.

22nd July 1993

The Very Revd W Roy SANDERSON
~ Former Moderator of the GENERAL ASSEMBLY
of the CHURCH OF SCOTLAND 1967 ~

In ecclesiastical affairs I personally did not have any contact with Cardinal Gray, though, like others in the Church of Scotland, I appreciated the leadership he gave to his own denomination and the courteous and, as far as he was able, the co-operative relationship he had with those of other communions especially, perhaps, the Church of Scotland.

On a personal basis, one time in the sixties when we both had been at some BBC function in Glasgow, we travelled back to Edinburgh in the train together. We did not discuss any weighty church matters but found a common bond in the fact that we each had been born in the Port of Leith. Certainly, the Cardinal was proud of being a Leither, as indeed I am myself.

Though our ways had not crossed when we were young, we had much to talk about and I recall that both of us as boys had enjoyed a circular tour (price 2d, all the way!) in an electric tram, which was a form of transport adopted by our native burgh long before Edinburgh! The tour went round by the docks, Newhaven, Granton and down the Ferry

Road, and the real enjoyment was to ride on the upper deck
of an open tram where the seats could be made to face either
way by switching the back-rest!

27th August 1993

The Very Revd Professor Thomas F TORRANCE
~ Former Moderator of the GENERAL ASSEMBLY
of the CHURCH OF SCOTLAND 1976 ~

Cardinal Gray was closely associated with the Order of
Christian Unity (Scotland) since its first meeting in
Edinburgh in 1977. He came regularly to our meetings,
and fully supported the aims of the Order regarding
Christian Education, the Christian Family and Christian
Principles in Medical Ethics.

He was very committed to Christian Unity at its deepest
level, a Christcentred Unity, and one which took seriously
the nature of the Church as none other than the Body of
Christ. While the Order itself is not concerned with working out doctrinal unity, it does rest squarely on Christian
belief in the Gospel as expressed in the Nicene Creed, and
is committed to acting it out in public and private life.
Cardinal Gray always brought to our meetings an aura of
unusual sanctity and compassion which seemed to give soul
to all we sought to do.

Recently, Cardinal Gray spoke of his joy in the fact that
both the Church of Scotland and the Roman Catholic Church
honoured the great John Duns Scotus as a theologian. As we
saw it, this indicated a depth of theological unity on which
we could continue to build.

Gordon Gray himself was above all a man of God with
great spiritual depth, who cared immensely for the pastoral
welfare of people, of whatever Christian allegiance.

My closest association with Gordon Gray was during my
year of service as Moderator of the General Assembly of the
Church of Scotland (1976-77). We worked together not

least in the Church/State Committee set up by the Under-Secretary of State which used to meet in the premises of the Scottish Office, in order to bring to the notice of the Government, matters of urgent social and public concern, usually in relation to education, of which Government ministers might not otherwise learn through official channels.

Representatives from most of the Scottish Churches participated, and their points of view were carefully noted. Cardinal Gray's presence contributed immeasurably to its harmony and success. His quiet authority and mature wisdom impressed us all, even the Synod Clerk of the Free Presbyterian Kirk!

That experience cemented for me a deep affection for him, which continued to grow whenever I discussed with him some troublesome matter affecting inter-Church relations or the personal need of someone known to us both. He was always ready to help anyone in need, and always treated them, however lowly he or she might be, as a dear child of God, one for whom Christ died and rose again. It was this mingling of deep evangelical concern with his episcopal office that particularly impressed me.

23rd September 1993

The Revd Robert WALKER
~ CHURCH OF SCOTLAND ~

The Church Leaders Forum owes its existence in no small measure to Cardinal Gray. It was he who encouraged, guided and supported Frank McElhone all those years ago when the idea was first proposed by him.

My own personal involvement with Gordon came about in that same event and it was at that time and later that I came to value his insights and respect his personal qualities. He was a great man, a true Christian, a convivial Scot and a friend to remember with joy.

20th July 1993

The Most Revd Derek WARLOCK,
Archbishop of Liverpool
~ CATHOLIC CHURCH ~

In his death, the Church has lost one of its great treasures.

He was revered for his warm humanity as well as his spiritual leadership and, of late, his very presence in Edinburgh, (although in retirement), provided great inspiration.

He was greatly respected in non-Catholic circles and proved a source of inspiration across the Border, where he will be remembered with affection.

23rd July 1993

The Revd Robert WATERS
~ SCOTTISH CONGREGATIONAL CHURCH ~

Gordon is dead. He is gone up with a shout, a cry of joy and thanksgiving which echoed around the heads of the great congregation in his favourite little cathedral church and soared heavenward, taking the heart-feelings of so many on the day his last wish was fulfilled and his body laid to rest.

It would be trite and superficial to say of Gordon that he could walk with kings, but keep the common touch. He would never be so patronising. More accurate to say that he could empathise with such grace as to be truly at one in any company, but never lose his own integrity.

The same was true in his handling of relationships between representatives of different Churches. He was well able to understand differences and close similarities, but his perspective was one which had no moving base.

His personal faith was the same base from which his official work was done. It was clearly founded on his conviction that his Church and its tradition supplied all that was needed for full discipleship. His Church had brought him to Christ: that was enough.

It was also the key to his understanding of spiritual, human and even Church administrative difficulties. He did not see them as problems, but as issues of faith, simple faith, and therefore capable of resolution. The thing that surprised so many was that as often as not this proved to be right.

He was a puzzle to many erudite church politicians who classed him as a tough conservative who made bald statements. A negotiator who didn't always speak their language. A man who had not moved with the times. Had they been trout fisherman they would have recognised when Gordon Gray was casting a fly and when they had, all unwitting, risen to it.

In discussion and argument, he showed an unexpected delicacy. There were those who thought they saw him perplexed in the face of hard decisions, but this was only because he saw so clearly the human cost of alternative courses of action.

He was actually a very soft-hearted man who tried to be tough when occasion demanded, but couldn't help being compassionate, like his Master, even when it did him no apparent good. There are too few like him in the world, never mind the church, whose greatness is not the world's gift, but always a green shoot of simplicity. Praise God for such a bonny friend.

19th December 1993

The Most Revd Thomas WINNING,
Archbishop of Glasgow
~ CATHOLIC CHURCH ~

When the history of the Scottish Catholic community in the second half of the twentieth century comes to be written, Cardinal Gordon Gray will shine out as a giant of the Christian faith.

A Scot to the very core of his being, his pride in the people of this country was mirrored by his fidelity to the Gospel and by his keen loyalty to the Holy Father.

Despite the high office he achieved within the Church, he never lost the common touch.

He was a much loved father-figure, a pastor graced with enormous sensitivity, and widely appreciated for his humanity, humility and prudence.

Gordon Joseph Gray was a man of faith and therefore a man of the people.

23rd July 1993

Index of Names